TODDLER LESSON PLANS:

Learning ABC's

Twenty-six week guide to help your toddler learn ABC's and numbers

Written by Autumn McKay

CREAT VE IDEAS PUBLISHING

Find me on Instagram!
@BestMomIdeas

Toddler Lesson Plans: Learning ABC's by Autumn McKay
Published by Creative Ideas Publishing

www.BestMomIdeas.com
© 2016 Autumn McKay

For permissions contact:
Permissions@BestMomIdeas.com

ISBN: 978-1-539886969

TABLE OF CONTENTS

My name is Autumn. I am a wife to an incredible husband, and a mother to two precious boys and a sweet little girl! My children are currently 6 years old, 4 years old and 2 years old.

I have a Bachelor of Science degree in Early Childhood Education. I have taught in the classroom and as an online teacher. I have earned teacher certifications to teach Kindergarten through Fifth grade in Colorado, California and Georgia. However, one of my greatest joys is being a mom! After my first son was born in 2013, I wanted to be involved in helping him learn and grow, so I began to develop color lessons to help engage his developing mind. I also wanted to help other moms dealing with hectic schedules and continuous time restraints. These activities evolved into my first book, called *Toddler Lesson Plans: Learning Colors*. I decided to continue the daily activities with my son, but this time we would focus on learning the alphabet and numbers which turned into *Toddler Lesson Plans: Learning ABC's*—the book you are currently holding. In addition, I created other activities that I have done with my children that eventually developed into another book titled *The Ultimate Toddler Activity Guide*. In preparing my oldest child for kindergarten I was motivated to write *The Ultimate Kindergarten Prep Guide*, which is full of many fun activities designed to prepare a preschooler for grade school

I have also developed a website called **BestMomIdeas.com**. It's a place where moms are encouraged to be the best version of themselves by feeling understood and never judged.

I hope that these resources will be as beneficial to you and your little ones, as they have been to my children and me!

LEARNING ABC'S

PLAY YOUR WAY TO LEARNING

Nothing is more charming than a child's face and the many expressions of joy a child exhibits in play and learning. Learning can be so fun! Playtime can be an enjoyable moment for the entire family. Throughout these pages, you will find many wonderful activities, which hold the potential to bring a smile to your child's face and joy in your home. My hope is that in the midst of your children "playing their way" to growth and knowledge, this book will help flood your home with joy.

As you begin your journey through this book, I need to mention that in most of the activities I address your child with the pronoun "he." I did this for simplicity and ease of writing; however, please know, as I wrote this book I was thinking of your precious little girl as well. I also want to reiterate that the goal of this book is to provide activities that you can enjoy with your child. The activities in this book are written for the preschooler. However, these years are a time of many developmental milestones. Each child is unique and matures at his or her own pace. If you sense your preschooler is becoming frustrated with an activity, please be sensitive and do not push your child to continue. **Without question, you know your child best and what he is capable of attempting.** If you feel an activity is beyond your child's present ability, simply move to another activity. There are many great "child tested" activities from which to choose.

Remember, even though significant learning will occur as you engage your child in these activities, I want you and your child to have fun! Often when my preschooler prays, he ends his prayer with the statement, "...And let us have a fun day, Amen." In the midst of hectic days and the constant pressure to perform, a child deserves a fun day. The truth is you deserve a "fun day" as well. It is my desire that in the following pages you will discover a path for your preschooler to learn, and an avenue through which you will experience immense satisfaction as YOU have a fun day and enjoy your child.

BENEFITS OF ACTIVITY TIME

Did you know that 90% of a child's brain develops by age 5? This means that almost all of a child's brain is developed before they enter kindergarten! With this in mind, it is important to actively engage your child in activities that are beneficial to your child's brain development.

"Activity time" refers to activating or stimulating a child's body and/or brain. This typically involves a hands-on experience for the preschooler where he is engaged in reading, running, climbing, coloring, pouring, etc.

Let me explain how the brain develops. When a baby is born, he is born with all the neurons (brain cells) that he will have for the rest of his life. It's the connections between the neurons that are crucial in brain development. A baby is born with very few connections. Connections, called synapses, are formed as a child is exposed to things around him. If the connections are used regularly, then they stay. However, if the connections aren't used, they are pruned and die.

Loving interactions with parents or caregivers help prepare a brain for learning. Every time you play, read, cook, garden, color, or do an educational activity with your child you are building connections in your child's developing brain. The more you do these activities the thicker these connections become in the brain. Clearly, activities are very important for the health and development of your child's brain. It would be appropriate to view the learning activities in this book as "brain food" for your child.

ADDITIONAL HELPFUL HINTS

Learning ABC's is an important step in learning to read. A child who can name all the letters in the alphabet will be equipped with an important foundation toward recognizing sounds and printed words. Having mastery of letter names can make learning letter sounds easier for children because the sound of the letter's name is often similar to the letter's sound.

This book includes activities for each letter of the alphabet. There is a table on the following pages that is an overview of all of the activities offered throughout the book. Six learning activities are available for each letter. Complete all six, or select those that you believe are most enjoyable and beneficial for your child. Once you select the letter to teach your child, turn to the corresponding page listed in the chart for a materials list and step-by-step instructions for each activity. Since a toddler's attention span is very short, the activities are designed to take 10 to 15 minutes. Nonetheless, do not be surprised if your child wants to repeat an activity several times. You will note that some activities are repeated for multiple letters. This should be helpful to you in being familiar with an activity, as well as being beneficial to your child.

Choose any letter to begin your learning journey. However I suggest focusing on one letter a week. Seeing the same letter repetitively each day for a week helps strengthen the connections in your toddler's brain. This will assist your child in remembering the letter and the letter's sound. Start with the first letter of the alphabet or start with letters that are familiar to your child. For example, you might want to select the letters that are in your child's name.

For each activity, I suggest that you ask your preschooler if he wants to do a fun activity. It is important that the learning experience is enjoyable. Some days, my children will tell me that they do not want to do an activity, and that is totally fine! However, on many days my children will take the initiative and ask me to do an activity with them. It makes this mommy's heart happy knowing that they want to learn!

I know many parents are very busy and have limited time to set up an activity. Consequently, I have placed a "low prep" ribbon beside all activities that take a minute or two to prep. I hope these low/no prep activities make life easier for you, especially on busy days.

To help you prepare your materials in advance, look ahead at the next set of activities you want to do with your toddler. At this time make a list of all the materials you need to buy during your next shopping trip to the grocery store. I try to keep an assortment of school supply items in my house to be used for activities, so I do not constantly have to run to the store. Here is a list of materials used consistently for many of the activities throughout this book:

- Construction Paper
- Glue
- Crayons
- Scissors (adult and toddler)
- Paper Plates
- Washable Paint
- Paintbrushes
- Markers
- Assortment of Stickers
- Food Coloring
- Pipe Cleaners

A GIFT FOR YOU

In appreciation of your purchase of this book, I am providing you with a link to the printable appendix pages. Giving you access to the appendix pages will allow you to have the appendix pages in color and your preschooler to do his favorite activity again and again.

www.BestMomIdeas.com/sendmyabcprintouts

Password: bestmomideas31a8

I hope these activities bring as much joy and learning to your home as they have mine!

UNIT OVERVIEW

	Monday	Tuesday	Wednesday	Thursday	Friday	Alternate Activity
Letter A	Apple Seed Counting*	Color Uppercase and Lowercase A's*	Apple Taste Test	Make an A for Alligator Picture*	Letter A Mystery Bag	Apple Printing
Letter B	Outline a B with Beans*	Make a B for Bunny Picture*	Bumblebee Matching	Make homemade bread and butter	Letter B mystery bag	Blow bubbles
Letter C	Make a C for Car Picture*	Read If you Give a Cat a Cupcake and Make Cupcakes*	Park Cars on the Correct Number	Sort Coins into Different Bowls*	Letter C Mystery Bag	Make Clouds
Letter D	Dot Shapes*	Dig for Dinosaurs*	Make a D for Duck Picture*	Feed the Dogs	Letter D Mystery Bag	Visit a Dog Shelter*
Letter E	Make Elephant Toothpaste	Make E for Elephant Picture*	Match Easter Eggs	Place Eggs in the Nest	Letter E Mystery Bag	Make an Elephant Mask
Letter F	Make a Fizzy Balloon	Flower Experiment	Five Green Frogs on a Log	Make F for Fox Picture*	Letter F Mystery Bag	Paint with Feathers*
Letter G	Outline a G with Grapes*	Make a Guitar	Make a G for Goat Picture	Make Green Goo*	Letter G Mystery Bag	Gravity Experiment*
Letter H	Make H for Horse Picture*	Paint a Hedgehog*	Match Helicopters	Find the Heart Number	Letter H Mystery Bag	Make Hedgehog Sandwiches
Letter I	Color a Picture of an Iguana*	Make I for Insect Picture*	Make an Igloo*	Make Insects in a Jar*	Letter I Mystery Bag	Make Ice Cream in a Bag*
Letter J	Make a J for Jellyfish Picture*	Play in Jello	Make a Jellyfish in a Jar	Make Jelly	Letter J Mystery Bag	Jumping J's*
Letter K	Make a Kite	Kick the Ball*	Make a K for Kangaroo Picture*	Make a Key*	Letter K Mystery Bag	Kitten Knitting*
Letter L	Make L for Ladybug Picture*	Make Lemonade*	Make a Lion Mask	Make a Lava Lamp	Letter L Mystery Bag	Lace the Letter L
Letter M	Magic Milk*	Make M for Mouse Picture*	Sort M&M's*	Read If you Give a Moose a Muffin and Make Muffins*	Letter M Mystery Bag	Make Maracas*

UNIT OVERVIEW

	Monday	Tuesday	Wednesday	Thursday	Friday	Alternate Activity
Letter N	Make a Necklace*	Play in Noodles	Make N for Night Picture*	Make Rice Krispy Treat Nests	Letter N Mystery Bag	Number Activity*
Letter O	Make O for Ostrich Picture*	Octopus Math*	Make Waffle Owls	O Stamping*	Letter O Mystery Bag	Otter Puppet*
Letter P	Make Pizza*	Make P for Penguin Picture*	Make Pom Pom Shooters	Paint with Popcorn	Letter P Mystery Bag	Find the Letter on the Pumpkin*
Letter Q	Trace Letters with a Q-Tip*	Make Quesadillas*	Play in Quicksand	Make Q for Quail Picture*	Letter Q Mystery Bag	Q-tip Shapes*
Letter R	Make Straw Rockets*	Make R for Rooster Picture*	Robot Size Order*	Rainbow Matching*	Letter R Mystery Bag	Make Rain in a Jar
Letter S	Make S for Snake Picture*	Paint Squiggles*	Star Counting	Make S'mores*	Letter S Mystery Bag	Shape Puzzle
Letter T	Name Train	Play Tennis*	Make T for Tree Picture*	Truck Patterns	Letter T Mystery Bag	Make a Turtle
Letter U	Utensil Painting*	Make U for Umbrella Picture*	Throw a Balloon Up*	U Toss	Letter U Mystery Bag	Learn Positions, like Under*
Letter V	Make Violins	Make a Volcano	Make V for Vulture Picture*	Vegetable Taste Test	Letter V Mystery Bag	Vacuum the Floor*
Letter W	Make a Windsock	Watermelon Counting*	Make W for Wagon Picture*	Make a Whale Snack	Letter W Mystery Bag	Make a Walrus Puppet
Letter X	X-ray Hands*	Make Xylophone Snack*	X Marks the Spot Patterns*	Make X for Xylophone Picture*	Letter X Mystery Bag	Paper Towel X-ray
Letter Y	Yarn Maze	Make Y for Yak Picture*	Make a Yo-Yo	Make Yogurt Drops*	Letter Y Mystery Bag	Wrap Yarn around *Y
Letter Z	Make Z for Zebra Picture*	Zip Jackets*	Zigzag race	Make a Zebra Mask*	Letter Z Mystery Bag	Zebra Tracks

The letter "A" makes two sounds—there is the long vowel sound that sounds like you are saying the letter "A," like "ay". And there is the short vowel sound that sounds like "ah." Most of these activities will focus on the short vowel sound.

MONDAY

LOW PREP *Apple Seed Counting*

Materials
- ☐ Apple Counting Activity Page (Appendix A)
- ☐ Black Beans

Directions

Explain to your toddler that the word "apple" starts with the letter A. Tell him the sound of the letter A. I tell my son the letter sound twice, and then say the word that starts with the letter, for example "*a, a, apple*." Next, explain to your toddler that apples have seeds on the inside; you can even cut an apple in half to show him the seeds.

From the *Apple Counting* activity page, show your toddler the numbers on the apples, and ask him to count with you as you point to the numbers on the apples. After you count together, tell your toddler to place the appropriate number of apple seeds on the apples. You will probably need to help your toddler place the correct number of apple seeds (black beans) on each apple. For example, your toddler will place one black bean on the number one apple. As you work through the activity together, ask him to tell you the first letter in the word "apple." Ask him to make the sound of the letter "A."

TUESDAY

LOW PREP *Coloring Upper and Lowercase A's*

Materials
- ☐ Upper and Lowercase A Activity Page (Appendix B)
- ☐ Green Crayon
- ☐ Red Crayon

Directions

Show your toddler the *Upper and Lowercase A* activity page. Tell him that the letter "A" can be big and point to the uppercase "A" on the activity page. Now tell him the letter "A" can be little and point to the lowercase "a" of the activity page. Ask your little one what sound the letter "A" makes. Tell your toddler that airplane starts with the letter "A". Tell him that he will color all of the big "A's" red. You can chose different colors if you wish. Hand him the red crayon and ask him to find the big "A's." Assist your child as needed. Once all of the uppercase "A's" are colored, hand your toddler the green crayon and ask him to color the lowercase "a's" green.

WEDNESDAY

Apple Taste Test

Materials

- ☐ 3 or 4 Different Types of Apples
- ☐ Plate
- ☐ Knife

Directions

Use the knife to cut the apples into slices—this is an adult job. Place one slice of each apple on a plate. Sit down with your toddler, and ask him to tell you the first letter in the word "apple." Ask your child if he can pronounce the sound of letter "A." Tell him that he will taste different kinds of apples. Have him pick out which apple he wants to try first. After he eats the apple slice, ask him if it was crunchy, sour, sweet, etc. Do this with each apple. After he tastes each apple, ask him which one was his favorite.

THURSDAY

LOW PREP ### Make an A for Alligator Picture

Materials

- ☐ Alligator Activity Page (Appendix C)
- ☐ Construction Paper
- ☐ Scissors
- ☐ Glue
- ☐ Crayons

Directions

Let your toddler color each part of the *Alligator* activity page. Cut out the pieces from the *Alligator* activity page. Ask your toddler to pick out a piece of construction paper on which to glue the alligator. Assemble the alligator, unglued, on the construction paper so your child can see an example of the finished product. Tell your toddler that alligator starts with the letter "A". Tell him the sound of the letter "A" and then say the word, alligator, for example, "*a, a, alligator*." Ask him to repeat it back to you. Ask your toddler to help rub glue on each piece of the alligator and press the pieces onto the construction paper. Assist your child as needed.

FRIDAY

Letter A Mystery Bag

Materials

- ☐ 4 Objects that Start with the Letter A (Ex. Apple, Airplane Puzzle Piece, Acorn)
- ☐ 4 Objects that Start with a Different Letter (Ex. Book, Key, Lemon)
- ☐ Duffle Bag

Directions

Place all eight objects in to the duffle bag. Tell your toddler that there are surprises in your bag. Explain to your child that some of the surprises start with the letter "A", and some surprises don't start with the letter "A." Ask him to reach into your bag and pull out one surprise. Ask him to tell you the name of the object. Now say the name of the object together with your child, and sound out the first letter of the object's name together. Ask your toddler if the object starts with the letter "A." If the object starts with the letter "A" put it in one pile. If the object does not start with the letter "A," place it in a different pile.

For example, if your toddler pulls out a book, ask him the name of the object. Next, say the word "book" together. Sound out the first letter of book to your toddler, like "*b, b, book*." Now ask him if the word "book" starts with the letter "A." After he answers, put the book in the "does not start with A" pile.

 # ALTERNATE ACTIVITY

Apple Printing

Materials

- ☐ Paper
- ☐ 1 Apple
- ☐ 2 Colors of Paint
- ☐ 2 Paper Plates
- ☐ Knife

Directions

First, cut the apple in half. You can cut it in half at the stem or along the middle. Put one half of the apple on each plate with each color of paint. Tell your toddler that he will be painting with apples. Ask your toddler to tell you the first letter of the word "apple", and then ask him what sound the letter "A" makes. Ask your child to dip the apple in the paint and stamp it onto the paper. After he is finished, let the painting dry, and assist him in hanging the painting in a special place.

LEARNING ABC'S

The letter "B" is a short sound made by a quick puff of air, "buh."

MONDAY

LOW PREP *Outline a B with Beans*

Materials

☐ B Activity Page (Appendix D)
☐ Elmer's Glue
☐ Bag of Beans—One Type or an Assortment

Directions

Using the *B* activity page show your toddler the letter B. Point to the uppercase "B" and tell him that is a big "B," and then point to the lowercase "b" and tell him that it is a little "b." Tell your toddler what sound a "B" makes, like "*b, b, beans*." Help your toddler trace the letters with his finger; this will help to develop his writing skills. Next, explain to your child that he will be gluing beans around the letter "B". Place a line of glue down the "B," and let your toddler start placing beans on the glue. Work in small sections, because it takes some time for his little hands to place the beans just right. As your little one is working, ask him what sound the letter "B" makes. When the picture is complete, let it dry, and then help your toddler hang it somewhere so he can continue to see it throughout the week.

TUESDAY

LOW PREP *Make a B for Bunny Picture*

Materials

☐ Bunny Activity Page (Appendix E)
☐ Cotton Balls
☐ Glue
☐ Scissors
☐ Construction Paper

Directions

Cut out the pieces from the *Bunny* activity page. Ask your toddler to pick out a piece of construction paper on which to glue the bunny. Assemble the bunny, unglued, on the construction paper so that your little one can see what the finished product should look like. Tell your toddler that bunny starts with the letter "B." Next, tell him the sound, "*b, b, bunny*." Ask him to repeat the letter and its sound back to you. Ask your toddler to rub glue on each piece of the bunny, and press the pieces onto the construction paper. Your child may need some assistance. Once the pieces are glued onto the construction paper, help your toddler glue cotton balls onto the "B" so you can have a fluffy bunny.

   LEARNING ABC'S

WEDNESDAY

Bumblebee Matching

Materials

☐ Bumblebee Activity Page (Appendix F)   ☐ Scissors

Directions

Cut out the bumblebees on the *Bumblebee* activity page. Next, cut the bumblebees in half where the uppercase "B" is on one half of the bumblebee and the lowercase "b" is on the other half. Explain to your toddler that he will be matching the big "B" with the little "b." Put all of the uppercase "B's" in a pile where each "B" is visible and do the same thing with the lowercase "b's." Ask your toddler what sound the letter "B" makes. You can tell him that the word bumblebee starts with the letter "B" and sound it out, "*b, b, bumblebee.*" Now ask your toddler to pick out an uppercase "B." Place that uppercase "B" in front of him, and ask him if he can find the lowercase "b" to match the uppercase "B." Once he finds it, put the two halves together and make the "*b, b, bumblebee*" sound together. Do this for each bumblebee. This activity will also help your toddler review his colors.

LOW PREP ### Make Bread and Butter

THURSDAY

Materials

☐ Mason Jar
☐ Heavy Whipping Cream
☐ Cooking Spray
☐ Loaf Pans or Cookie Sheet
☐ 2 Cups of Hot Water
☐ ½ Cup Light Virgin Olive Oil
☐ ¼ Cup of Honey

☐ 4 Teaspoons of Instant Yeast
☐ 1 Egg
☐ 5 Cups Wheat Flour
☐ 2 Teaspoons of Salt
☐ 2 Tablespoons of Lecithin (Makes the Bread Less Dense)
☐ ½ Teaspoon of Gluten (Optional)

Directions

Let your toddler help you pour all of the ingredients into a mixer in the following manner. First, combine water, oil, honey, and the egg. Start mixing it together in the mixer (I use the mixing hook of the Kitchen Aid Mixer). While you are mixing add 3 cups of flour, and the yeast, salt, lecithin, and gluten. Mix well. Add in the other 2 cups of flour. After the dough is mixed together, pull half of the dough from the bowl and set it in another bowl. Turn the mixer to the next to last speed and knead for 8-9 minutes—it should be a nice ball. Set this dough aside and do the same kneading process with the other half of the dough. Grease your loaf pans, and shape your dough balls into loaves and place the dough in the loaf pans. Both halves will need to rise until they are doubled—it usually takes about 45 minutes. If you are making rolls, you can break the dough balls apart into small balls and place on a greased cookie sheet to rise until they are doubled—it usually takes about 45 minutes. Bake the bread at 350 degrees Fahrenheit for 30 minutes for loaves and 25 minutes for rolls.

Recipe adapted from Breadbeckers.

To make the butter, fill your mason jar half full of room temperature heavy whipping cream. Add a squirt of honey if you want to make honey butter. Then comes the fun part for your little one, as you ask him to shake it as hard as he can until the cream turns to butter. You can then enjoy some homemade butter on your homemade bread! As you are making bread and butter together, tell your toddler what letter bread and butter start with and what sound the letter "B" makes. Sound out the beginning of the words, "*b, b, bread*" and "*b, b, butter.*"

FRIDAY

Letter B Mystery Bag

Materials

- ☐ 4 Objects that Start with the Letter B (Ex. Book, Ball, Banana)
- ☐ 4 Objects that Start with a Different Letter (Ex. Apple, Car, Screwdriver)
- ☐ Duffle Bag

Directions

Put all eight objects in to the duffle bag. Tell your toddler that there are surprises in your bag. Explain that some surprises start with the letter "B," and some surprises don't start with the letter "B." Ask him to reach into your bag and pull out one surprise. Ask him what the object is that he pulled out. Say the name of the object together with your child, and sound out the first letter of the object's name together. Ask your toddler if the object starts with the letter "B." If it does start with a "B," put it in one pile, but if the object does not start with the letter "B" put it in a different pile.

For example, if your toddler pulls out a book. Ask him the name of the object. Next you would say "book" together. Sound out the first letter of book to your toddler, like "*b, b, book.*" Then ask him if book starts with "B." After he answers, put the book in the "does start with B" pile.

ALTERNATE ACTIVITY

LOW PREP *Blow Bubbles*

Materials

- ☐ Bottle of Bubbles

Directions

Using a bottle of bubbles go outside and blow bubbles with your little one. As you blow bubbles together, tell him that bubbles starts with the letter "B," and sound it out for him "*b, b, bubbles.*" Ask your toddler to repeat it back to you.

The letter "C" has two sounds. It makes a "k" sound and a "s" sound. Focus on teaching your toddler the "k" sound.

MONDAY

LOW PREP *Make a C for Car Picture*

Materials

- ☐ Car Activity Page (Appendix G)
- ☐ Scissors
- ☐ Glue
- ☐ Construction Paper
- ☐ Crayons

Directions

Let your toddler color each part of the *Car* activity page. Cut out the pieces from the *Car* activity page. Ask your toddler to pick out a piece of construction paper on which to glue the car and road. Assemble the car and road, unglued, on the construction paper so your little one can see what the finished product should look like. Tell your toddler that the word "car" starts with the letter "C." Now tell him the sound, "*c, c, car.*" Ask him to repeat it back to you. Ask your toddler to help rub glue on each piece of the road and car, and press the pieces onto the construction paper. Your child may need some assistance. After the car is complete, find a place to hang the picture so that your little one can be proud of his work.

TUESDAY

LOW PREP *Read If You Give a Cat a Cupcake and Make Cupcakes*

Materials

- ☐ If You Give a Cat a Cupcake
- ☐ Cupcake Mix and Ingredients from Box
- ☐ Frosting
- ☐ Sprinkles (Optional)
- ☐ Muffin Pan
- ☐ Cupcake Liners
- ☐ Bowl
- ☐ Spoon

Directions

Buy the book, **If You Give a Cat a Cupcake**, or check it out from the library. Most toddlers like to hold the book and flip through the pages as you read, but you may also listen to someone read the story online. After you read the story together tell your little one that the word "cat" starts with the letter "C" and the word "cupcake" starts with the letter "C." Sound out both words for your child, "*c, c, cat*" and "*c, c, cupcake.*" Next, make cupcakes together. Follow the directions from the box of cupcake mix. Let you toddler assist you by pouring the ingredients into the bowl, stirring, and placing the cupcake liners in the muffin pan. As you are baking, ask your toddler what letter cupcake starts with, and see if he can tell you what sound the letter "C" makes. Don't forget to frost your cupcakes after they cool and add some fun sprinkles. Enjoy!

LEARNING ABC'S

WEDNESDAY

Park Cars on the Correct Number

Materials

- ☐ 10-20 Toy Cars
- ☐ Circle Labeling Stickers
- ☐ Post-It Notes
- ☐ Marker
- ☐ Masking Tape

Directions

Ask your toddler if he would like to park cars. Tell him that the word "car" starts with the letter "C." Ask him if he knows the sound of the letter "C.". Sound it out together, "c, c, car." Work on counting 1-10 or 1-20. My son loved this activity so much that he wanted to count 1-20. All you need to do is write out the numbers 1-20 on Post-It Notes. There should be one number for each Post-It Note. Place the Post-It Notes in order along the floor in a straight line (I placed them at the edge of the fireplace). Place a piece of masking tape in between each number to make it look like parking spots for the cars. Next you will need to number the circle labeling stickers with numbers 1-20. There should be one number for each sticker. Place one label on each car. Now explain to your toddler that he will drive the cars and park them in the matching number parking spot. It may be helpful to show your child an example by taking the number 1 car and driving it to the number 1 parking spot. After he parks all of the cars, count the cars together in order.

LOW PREP ## Sort Coins

Materials

- ☐ Assorted Coins (Pennies, Nickels, Dimes, and Quarters)
- ☐ 5 bowls or cups

Directions

Place four bowls in front of your toddler. Next, show him a bowl full of assorted coins. Tell him that they are coins. Tell him that coins starts with the letter "C," and sound it out for him, "c, c, coins." Ask him to repeat it back to you. Show him that he is going to be sorting coins. Place a penny in one bowl, and tell him all of the pennies will go in that bowl. Do the same for each coin. You might have to assist him. Be sure to praise him as he correctly places the coins in the appropriate bowl.

THURSDAY

   LEARNING ABC'S

FRIDAY

Letter C Mystery Bag

Materials

- ☐ 4 Objects that Start with the Letter C (Ex. Car, Cup, Coin)
- ☐ 4 Objects that Start with a Different Letter (Ex. Balloon, Marker, Rattle)
- ☐ Duffle Bag

Directions

Put all eight objects in to the duffle bag. Tell your toddler that there are surprises in your bag. Explain that some surprises start with the letter "C," and some surprises don't start with the letter "C." Ask him to reach into your bag and pull out one surprise. Ask him what the object is that he pulled out. Say the name of the object together, and sound out the first letter of the object's name together. Ask your toddler if the object starts with "C." If it does start with a "C," then put it in one pile, but if it doesn't start with the letter "C" put it in a different pile.

For example, if your toddler pulls out a car. Ask him the name of the object. Next, you would say "car" together. Sound out the first letter of car to your toddler, "c, c, car." Now ask him if car starts with "C." After he answers, put the car in the "does start with C" pile.

 ## ALTERNATE ACTIVITY

Make Clouds

Materials

- ☐ Muffin Pan
- ☐ Whipped Cream
- ☐ Marshmallow Fluff
- ☐ Marshmallows
- ☐ Coconut Oil
- ☐ White Sprinkles
- ☐ Cookie Sheet

Directions

Place all of the edible materials into the muffin pan cups. Explain to your toddler that he will be making clouds out of these materials. Tell him that clouds start with the letter "C," and sound it out for him, "c, c, clouds." You can even go to the window and look at clouds before you start the activity. Ask your little one to feel each item and describe how it feels (sticky, soft, squishy, etc.). Now tell him that he can use his hands to make a cloud on the cookie sheet. It is a good to dip your finger in the whipped cream and show him how to get started. As he is making his clouds ask him to tell you what sound the letter "C" makes.

Use your tongue to push against the roof of your mouth as you make the "duh" sound for letter "D."

MONDAY

LOW PREP *Dot Shapes*

Materials

- ☐ Circle Labeling Stickers
- ☐ Paper
- ☐ Marker

Directions

On the piece of paper draw pictures of different shapes (circle, square, rectangle, diamond, etc.). Explain to your toddler that he will use the dot stickers to outline the shapes. Tell your toddler that dot starts with the letter "D". Sound out the letter "D" for him, "*d, d, dot*." Ask him to repeat it back to you. Hand him one sticker at a time and ask him to place it on the shape.

LOW PREP *Dig for Dinosaurs*

Materials

- ☐ 6 Plastic Dinosaurs
- ☐ Big Bag of Uncooked Rice
- ☐ Plastic Bin
- ☐ Shovel

Directions

Dump your big bag of rice into your plastic bin. Bury the plastic dinosaurs in the rice. If you are unable to purchase the dinosaurs, you can print off some pictures of dinosaurs to bury in the rice. Show your toddler the bin of rice and tell him that he will be digging for dinosaurs. Tell your toddler that dinosaur starts with the letter "D." Ask him what sound the letter "D" makes. Sound out dinosaur together, "*d, d, dinosaur*." Let your little one use the shovel to dig out the dinosaurs. He will probably want to do this activity a few times.

TUESDAY

WEDNESDAY

LOW PREP *Make a D for Duck Picture*

Materials

- ☐ Duck Activity Page (Appendix H)
- ☐ Construction Paper
- ☐ Glue
- ☐ Scissors
- ☐ Crayons

Directions

Let your toddler color each part of the *Duck* activity page. Cut out the pieces from the *Duck* activity page. Ask your toddler to pick out a piece of construction paper on which to glue the duck. Assemble the duck, unglued, on the construction paper so your little one can see what the finished product should look like. Tell your toddler that duck starts with the letter "D." Tell him the sound in this manner, "*d, d, duck.*" Ask him to repeat it back to you. Ask your toddler to help rub glue on each piece of the duck, and press the pieces onto the construction paper. Assist your child as needed. After the duck is complete, find a place to hang the picture so your little one can be proud of his work.

THURSDAY

Feed the Dogs

Materials

- ☐ Dog Activity Pages (Appendix I)
- ☐ 2 Paper Lunch Bags
- ☐ Glue
- ☐ Scissors
- ☐ Marker

Directions

Cut out the pieces of the *Dog* activity pages. Glue one dog face on each paper lunch bag. Cut out the mouth of the dog so that the bones will fit in the mouth. Label one bag with an uppercase "D" and the other bag with a lowercase "d." Mix up the upper and lowercase "D" bones. Tell your little one that he will be feeding the dogs. Tell him that dog starts with the letter "D." Ask him if he knows what sound the letter "D" makes. Sound out the word "dog" together, "*d, d, dog.*" Show your toddler that the uppercase "D's" will be fed to the uppercase "D" dog, and the lowercase "d's" will be fed to the lowercase "d" dog. Be sure to praise him when he does it correctly.

LEARNING ABC'S

FRIDAY

Letter D Mystery Bag

Materials

- ☐ 4 Objects that Start with the Letter D (Ex. Dinosaur, Diaper, Dog)
- ☐ 4 Objects that Start with a Different Letter (Ex. Apple, Spoon, Yo-yo)
- ☐ Duffle Bag

Directions

Put all eight objects in to the duffle bag. Tell your toddler that there are surprises in your bag. Explain that some surprises start with the letter "D," and some surprises don't start with the letter "D." Ask him to reach into your bag and pull out one surprise. Ask him what the object is that he pulled out. Say the name of the object together, and sound out the first letter of the object's name together. Ask your toddler if the object starts with "D." If the object starts with a "D," put it in one pile, but if it doesn't put it in a different pile.

For example, if your toddler pulls out a yo-yo. Ask him the name of the object. Next, you would say "yo-yo" together. Sound out the first letter of yo-yo to your toddler, "*y, y, yo-yo.*" Now ask him if yo-yo starts with "D." After he answers, put the yo-yo in the "does not start with D" pile.

ALTERNATE ACTIVITY

LOW PREP Visit a Dog Shelter

Materials

- ☐ Dog Shelter
- ☐ Dog Treats (Optional)

Directions

Contact your local animal shelter and ask if you can bring your toddler to visit some dogs. I'd also ask if you can bring treats to share with the dogs.

The letter "E" has a short vowel sound, "eh" and a long vowel sound, "ee." These activities focus on teaching the short vowel sound.

MONDAY

Make Elephant Toothpaste

Materials

- ☐ ½ Cup of Hydrogen Peroxide
- ☐ 1 Teaspoon of Yeast
- ☐ 2 Tablespoons of Hot Water
- ☐ Food Coloring
- ☐ 2-3 Tablespoons of Dish Soap
- ☐ Empty Water Bottle
- ☐ Tray on Which to Stand the Water Bottle
- ☐ Funnel (Optional)
- ☐ Small Dish

Directions

Excite your toddler by telling him you will be making elephant toothpaste today! Tell him that elephants have big teeth and need a lot of toothpaste. (Elephants typically have 26 teeth—the 2 incisors, which are also known as the tusks, 12 deciduous premolars, and 12 molars). Tell your little one that the word elephant starts with the letter "E," and he will be learning about the letter "E" this week. Sound it out for him, "*e, e, elephant.*" Ask your toddler to say the sound with you.

To do the activity, first pour the yeast into a small dish and add hot water. Stir it thoroughly. Next, place the funnel in the empty bottle so your toddler can pour the peroxide into the bottle without making a mess. Ask your toddler to pick a color of food coloring to pour into the bottle, and let him squirt some into the bottle. Add your dish soap to the bottle. Now add the yeast mixture to the bottle. Notice your toddler's eyes as he watches what happens. Let him squeeze the bottle, play in the toothpaste, or just admire his work.

TUESDAY

LOW PREP ## Make an E for Elephant Picture

Materials

- ☐ Elephant Activity Page (Appendix J)
- ☐ Scissors
- ☐ Glue
- ☐ Construction Paper
- ☐ Crayons

Directions

Let your toddler color each part of the *Elephant* activity page. Cut out the pieces from the *Elephant* activity page. Ask your toddler to pick out a piece of construction paper on which to glue the elephant. Assemble the elephant, unglued, on the construction paper so that your little one can see what the finished product should look like. Tell your toddler that elephant starts with the letter "E." Next, tell him the sound, "*e, e, elephant.*" Ask him to repeat it back to you. Ask your toddler to help rub glue on each piece of the elephant, and press the pieces onto the construction paper—he may need some assistance. After the elephant is complete, find a place to hang the picture so that your little one can be proud of his work. In my family, we started building an alphabet wall in our house, so my son could see previous letters and new letters each week.

LEARNING ABC'S

WEDNESDAY

Match Easter Eggs

Materials

- ☐ 8 Plastic Eggs
- ☐ Marker

Directions

Write an uppercase "E" on the top half of each plastic egg. Next, write a lowercase "e" on the bottom half of each plastic egg. Split the eggs apart. Tell your toddler that he will be matching the uppercase "E" with the Lowercase "e." Show him how to match the eggs together. Tell your child that egg starts with the letter "E," and sound it out for them, "*e, e, egg.*" Ask your toddler to make the "E" sound when he finds a match.

THURSDAY

Place Eggs in the Nest

Materials

- ☐ Nest Activity Page (Appendix K)
- ☐ Counters
- ☐ Scissors

Directions

Explain to your toddler that birds build a nest for their home and they lay eggs in the nest. You can tell them that the mommy bird takes really good care of the eggs until the baby bird hatches out of the egg. Ask your toddler what letter the word "egg" starts with, and ask him if he can tell you the sound that the letter "E" makes.

Using the *Nest* activity pages, show your toddler the numbers on the nests, and ask him to count with you as you point to the numbers on the nests. After you count together, tell your toddler that he will now be putting eggs in the nests. You can use counters, marbles, beans, etc. as your eggs. Tell your little one that he needs to place the same number of eggs in the nest that matches the number on the picture. For example, your toddler will place one counter on the number one nest. (I ask my son to tell me the number on the nest, then we count out that many counters together, and he places all of the eggs into the nest.)

FRIDAY

Letter E Mystery Bag

Materials

- ☐ 4 Objects that Start with the Letter E (Ex. Easter Egg, Envelope, Eraser)
- ☐ 4 Objects that Start with a Different Letter (Ex. Movie, Ball, Yo-yo)
- ☐ Duffle Bag

Directions

Put all eight objects in to the duffle bag. Tell your toddler that there are surprises in your bag. Explain that some surprises start with the letter "E," and some surprises don't start with the letter "E." Ask him to reach into your bag and pull out one surprise. Ask him what the object is that he pulled out. Say the name of the object together, and sound out the first letter of the object's name together. Ask your toddler if the object starts with "E." If it does start with an "E," then put it in one pile, but if it does not put it in a different pile.

For example, if your toddler pulls out a yo-yo. Ask him the name of the object. Next, pronounce the word with your child, "yo-yo." Sound out the first letter of yo-yo to your toddler, "*y, y, yo-yo.*" Now ask him if yo-yo starts with "E." After he answers, put the yo-yo in the "does not start with E" pile.

ALTERNATE ACTIVITY

Make an Elephant Mask

Materials

- ☐ Gray Crayon or Paint
- ☐ Gray Construction Paper
- ☐ Paper Plate
- ☐ Glue
- ☐ Scissors
- ☐ Popsicle Stick (Optional)
- ☐ Tape

Directions

Ask your toddler if he would like to make an elephant mask. Tell him that he can be an elephant for the day. Ask him if he knows what letter elephant starts with, and then ask if he knows what sound the letter "E" makes. Sound the letter out together, "e, e, *elephant.*" To make the mask, ask your toddler to color or paint the paper plate gray. If you paint the plate, you will have to wait for it to dry before going to the next step.

After the plate is dry, cut two holes in the plate for eyes. Next, cut a long strip from your gray construction paper; it should be about an inch wide and as long as the longest side of the construction paper. This strip of paper will be the elephant's trunk. Help your toddler fold the strip of paper like an accordion—going back and forth and glue one end of the nose to the center of the plate. Cut out the ears from the gray construction paper. The ears should look a lot like the shape of butterfly wings, but you can cut ovals if that is easier. Glue the ears on the sides of the plate. Now you can tape a popsicle stick to the bottom, backside of the plate so your toddler is able to hold the mask up to his face, but that is optional. Enjoy your little elephant!

To create the letter "F" sound the jaw is nearly closed and air is pushed out of the mouth between the top teeth and bottom lip, "f."

MONDAY

Make a Fizzy Balloon

Materials

- ☐ Empty Water Bottle
- ☐ ½ Cup of Vinegar
- ☐ 1 Tablespoon of Baking Soda
- ☐ Funnel
- ☐ Balloon

Directions

Ask your toddler if he wants to make a fizzy balloon. I'm sure he will say yes! Tell him that he will be learning about the letter "F" this week, and the word fizzy starts with the letter "F." Make the sound for him, "*f, f, fizzy.*" Ask him to repeat the sound. Now have your toddler pick out a balloon. Use the funnel to put one tablespoon of baking soda into the balloon. Shake it gently to move all of the baking soda to the bottom of the balloon. Use your funnel to let your toddler help you pour the vinegar into the empty bottle. Stretch the open end of the balloon over the neck of the bottle, but try to make sure no baking soda falls into the bottle. Hold the bottle while you let your little one lift the balloon so the baking soda falls into the bottle. (Be sure to have a lot of balloons on hand because I'm sure your little one will want to do this activity multiple times like my son did!)

TUESDAY

Flower Experiment

Materials

- ☐ White Flowers (Carnations, Roses, Daises, etc.- I purchased some flowers on clearance at a local grocery store)
- ☐ Food Coloring
- ☐ Glasses or Vases
- ☐ Scissors
- ☐ Water

Directions

My son and I enjoyed this experiment all week! Tell your toddler that you will be doing an experiment with flowers today, and will continue to watch them during the week. Tell your toddler that flowers start with the letter "F." Sound it out for them, "*f, f, flower.*" Ask him to say it with you. Begin by trimming the flowers down so they will fit in your glasses or vases. Let your toddler pick out four food colors to use; you can do more, but we just did four. Fill your glasses or vases with water, and then let your little one add a few drops of food coloring to each glass or vase. It should be one color per glass. Next, ask your toddler to add a flower or two to each glass. Place the flowers in a nice sunny spot. (We kept ours on the kitchen table.) Ask your toddler what he thinks will happen to the flowers. If you give the flowers a fresh trim each day, they will drink a little more water and change color a little faster. Our flowers stared changing colors in approximately two hours. It was very fun to watch!

WEDNESDAY

Five Green Frogs on a Log

Materials

- ☐ Frog Activity Page (Appendix L)
- ☐ Scissors
- ☐ Tape
- ☐ Popsicle Sticks
- ☐ Paper Towel Tube

Directions

Cut out the frogs on the activity page and tape them to a popsicle stick. Now cut the paper towel tube in half—long ways. Open the tube up and place the tube on the counter or floor. This will become your log for the frogs. Now you need to cut five slits in the log so the popsicle sticks can fit in them. Place the frogs on the log. Now ask your toddler if he would like to sing a song with the frogs. Tell your toddler that frog starts with the letter "F." Sound it out for him, "f, f, frog." Ask him to repeat it back to you. Sing the song to them:

Five little speckled frogs,
sitting on a mossy log.
Eating the most delicious bugs.
Yum! Yum!
One jumped into the pool,
where it was nice and cool.
Now there are four speckled frogs.

After singing the song a few times your child will probably join in at some point. At the end of the song have your toddler take the fifth frog off the log, so he can see that there are four frogs remaining on the log. This will continue until there are no speckled frogs remaining on the log. (My son enjoyed the song so much he made me sing it for two days. Be prepared!)

LOW PREP Make an F for Fox Picture

Materials

- ☐ Fox Activity Page (Appendix M)
- ☐ Scissors
- ☐ Glue
- ☐ Construction Paper
- ☐ Crayons

Directions

Let your toddler color each part of the *Fox* activity page. Cut out the pieces from the *Fox* activity page. Ask your toddler to pick out a piece of construction paper on which to glue the fox. Assemble the fox, unglued, on the construction paper so that your little one can see what the finished product should look like. Tell your toddler that the word fox starts with the letter "F." Next, tell him the sound, "f, f, fox." Ask him to repeat it back to you. Ask your toddler to help rub glue on each piece of the fox, and press the pieces onto the construction paper—he may need some assistance. After the fox is complete, find a place to hang the picture so that your little one can be proud of their work. (We added it to our alphabet wall.)

THURSDAY

LEARNING ABC'S

FRIDAY

Letter F Mystery Bag

Materials

- ☐ 4 Objects that Start with the Letter F (Ex. Feather, Flower, Flashlight)
- ☐ 4 Objects that Start with a Different Letter (Ex. Goldfish, Book, Crayon)
- ☐ Duffle Bag

Directions

Put all eight objects in to the duffle bag. Tell your toddler that there are surprises in your bag. Explain that some surprises start with the letter F, and some surprises don't start with the letter "F." Ask him to reach into your bag and pull out one surprise. Ask him what the object is that he pulled out. Say the name of the object together, and sound out the first letter of the object's name together. Ask your toddler if the object starts with "F." If it does start with an "F," put it in one pile, but if it doesn't put it in a different pile.

For example, if your toddler pulls out a flashlight. Ask him the name of the object. Next, you would say "flashlight" together. Sound out the first letter of flashlight to your toddler, "*f, f, flashlight.*" Now ask him if flashlight starts with F. After he answers, put the flashlight in the "does start with F" pile.

 # ALTERNATE ACTIVITY

LOW PREP *Paint with Feathers*

Materials

- ☐ Paper
- ☐ Feathers
- ☐ Paint
- ☐ Paper Plate

Directions

Tell your toddler that he will have the opportunity to paint with feathers today. Ask him if he knows the first letter in the word "feather." Next, ask him if he knows what sound the letter "F" makes. You can sound out feathers with him if he needs some help, "*f, f, feathers.*" It would be helpful to have one feather for each color paint he is using so the paints do not get mixed together. Pour some paint onto the paper plate and place a feather in each paint color. Let your toddler have fun creating a feather painting!

   LEARNING ABC'S

The letter "G" has two sounds. The first sound is a hard sound and makes the sound "guh." The second sound is a soft sound that makes the sound "juh" like the letter "J."

MONDAY

LOW PREP *Outline a G with Grapes*

Materials

- ☐ Paper
- ☐ Marker
- ☐ Grapes

Directions

Draw a big uppercase "G" on a piece of paper. Draw a big lowercase "g" on the paper. Tell your toddler that he will be learning about the letter "G" this week. Tell him that he will use grapes to outline the letter "G" today. Tell your little one that the word grape starts with the letter "G". Sound it out for him, "*g, g, grapes.*" Ask him to repeat the sound back to you. After he outlines the "G," he can enjoy a nice snack.

TUESDAY

Make a Guitar

Materials

- ☐ Rectangle Tissue Box or Cereal Box
- ☐ Scissors
- ☐ Marker
- ☐ Big Rubber Bands
- ☐ Paper Towel Tube
- ☐ Tape
- ☐ Stickers, Paint, or Crayons

Directions

Ask your toddler if he would like to make a guitar today. Tell your toddler that the word guitar starts with the letter "G." Sound it out for him, "*g, g, guitar.*" Ask your toddler if he can sound out guitar. If you are using a cereal box, cut out an oval on the front of the cereal box just like a guitar. Next, trace the paper towel tube on the top of your box. After you trace the tube, cut the circle out of the box for your toddler to slide the paper towel tube inside the hole. This is your guitar handle. Put tape around the tube so that the tube doesn't slide out.

Now, decorate the guitar with stickers, paint, crayons or whatever he would like. After he decorates his guitar, ask him to help you slide rubber bands around the box. The rubber bands should go along the length of the box—top to bottom of the box. Enjoy the beautiful music your toddler plays for you!

 LEARNING ABC'S

WEDNESDAY

LOW PREP *Make a G for Goat Picture*

Materials

- ☐ Goat Activity Page (Appendix N)
- ☐ Scissors
- ☐ Glue
- ☐ Construction Paper
- ☐ Crayons

Directions

Let your toddler color each part of the *Goat* activity page. Cut out the pieces from the *Goat* activity page. Ask your toddler to pick out a piece of construction paper on which to glue the goat. Assemble the goat, unglued, on the construction paper so your little one can see what the finished product should look like. Tell your toddler the word goat starts with the letter "G." Then tell him the sound, "*g, g, goat.*" Ask him to repeat it back to you. Ask your toddler to help rub glue on each piece of the goat, and press the pieces onto the construction paper. Your child may need some assistance. After the goat is complete, find a place to hang the picture so your little one can be proud of his work. (We added it to our alphabet wall.)

THURSDAY

LOW PREP *Make Green Goo*

Materials

- ☐ 4 oz of Elmer's Glue
- ☐ 1 Cup of Water and 1/3 Cup of Water
- ☐ 2 Teaspoons of Borax
- ☐ Green Food Coloring
- ☐ 2 Bowls
- ☐ Spoon

Directions

Ask your toddler if he wants to make green goo. Ask him if he can tell you the first letter of the words "green" and "goo." Ask him if he can tell you what sound the letter "G" makes. Sound it out with him, "*g, g, green*" and "*g, g, goo.*" Ask your toddler to pour the glue into the bowl, and then have them pour one cup of water in with the glue. Mix it together. Ask your little one to put some green food coloring in the mixture. Ask him to tell you what letter the word green starts with. In a separate bowl, mix Borax with 1/3 cup of warm water. Have your child stir the mixture until it's dissolved. Now mix both bowls together. Let your toddler enjoy playing in his green goo!

FRIDAY

Letter G Mystery Bag

Materials

☐ 4 Objects that Start with the Letter G (Ex. Green Crayon, Goat, Goldfish)
☐ 4 Objects that Start with a Different Letter (Ex. Apple, Water Bottle, Jacket)
☐ Duffle Bag

Directions

Put all eight objects in to the duffle bag. Tell your toddler that there are surprises in your bag. Explain that some surprises start with the letter "G," and some surprises don't start with the letter "G." Ask him to reach into your bag and pull out one surprise. Ask him what the object is that he pulled out. Say the name of the object together with your child, and sound out the first letter of the object's name together. Ask your toddler if the object starts with "G." If it does start with a "G," then put it in one pile, but if it doesn't put it in a different pile.

For example, if your toddler pulls out a green crayon. Ask him the name of the object. Next, you would say "green crayon" together. Sound out the first letter of green crayon to your toddler, "g, g, green." Now ask him if green crayon starts with "G." After he answers, put the green crayon in the "does start with G" pile.

ALTERNATE ACTIVITY

LOW PREP *Gravity Experiment*

Materials

☐ Any Number of Balls of Varying Sizes and Weights

Directions

Tell your toddler that he is going to learn about gravity today. Tell him that gravity starts with the letter "G." Make the sound for him, "g, g, gravity." Ask him to say it too. You can tell him that gravity is what keeps his feet on the ground and it's what makes things fall to the ground. Ask your little one to jump up. Tell him it was gravity that pulled him back to the ground. Show your toddler all of the balls you have collected, and tell him that you will drop two balls at the same time to see which one hits the ground first. For the bigger balls you can hold one ball while your toddler holds the other. Make sure that the balls are at the same height and are dropped at the same time. You may need to practice a few times. If it doesn't seem to be working, try pushing the balls off the edge of the kitchen table at the same time. Each time you do a ball drop ask your toddler which ball hit the ground first or if they hit at the same time (they should hit at the same time).

LEARNING ABC'S

The letter "H" sound does not have a specific mouth shape, simply breathe out through your mouth.

MONDAY

LOW PREP *Make an H for Horse Picture*

Materials

- ☐ Horse Activity Page (Appendix O)
- ☐ Scissors
- ☐ Glue
- ☐ Construction Paper
- ☐ Crayons

Directions

Let your toddler color each part of the *Horse* activity page. Cut out the pieces from the *Horse* activity page. You will need to cut slits ¾ the way down in the horse's mane. Ask your toddler to pick out a piece of construction paper on which to glue the horse. Assemble the horse, unglued, on the construction paper so that your little one can see what the finished product should look like. Tell your toddler that horse starts with the letter "H." Next, tell him the sound, "*h, h, horse.*" Ask him to repeat it back to you. Ask your toddler to help rub glue on each piece of the horse, and press the pieces onto the construction paper. You child may need some assistance. After the horse is complete, find a place to hang the picture so your little one can be proud of his work. (We added it to our alphabet wall.)

TUESDAY

LOW PREP *Paint a Hedgehog*

Materials

- ☐ Hedgehog Activity Page (Appendix P)
- ☐ Brown Paint
- ☐ Plastic Fork
- ☐ Paper Plate

Directions

Tell your toddler that he will get to paint spikes on a hedgehog today. Show him the picture of the hedgehog on the activity page. Tell your little one that the word hedgehog starts with the letter "H." Next, make the sound for him, "*h, h, hedgehog.*" Ask him to say it with you. Place brown paint on the paper plate. Show your toddler how to dip the prongs of the fork into the paint, and stamp the fork onto the hedgehog to make spikes. Let him add as many spikes as he would like. When he is finished, be sure to let the paint dry before hanging his masterpiece on your wall.

WEDNESDAY

Match Helicopters

Materials

- ☐ Helicopter Activity Page (Appendix Q)
- ☐ Scissors

Directions

Cut out the helicopters from the *Helicopter* activity page. After cutting out each helicopter, cut them in half. Explain to your toddler that he will match the front and back of the helicopters together. Show him how to match the same color together. The red back and the red front will go together. Tell your little one that the word helicopter starts with the letter "H." Ask him if he knows what sound the letter "H" makes. Sound out helicopter with your child, "*h, h, helicopter.*"

Find the Heart Number

THURSDAY

Materials

- ☐ Construction Paper
- ☐ Marker
- ☐ Small Pieces of Construction Paper

Directions

Draw a big heart on a piece of construction paper. Inside the heart write numbers 1-10 or 1-20 in random places. Draw a heart around each number. Tear up pieces of construction paper so your toddler can place a piece of paper over the number you call out. Show your toddler the activity, and explain that he will be finding numbers. Ask him to tell you the shape the numbers are in. Tell him the word heart starts with the letter "H." Ask your little one if he knows what sound the letter "H" makes. Sound it out together, "*h, h, heart.*" Now call out numbers for him to locate. When he locates the number, have your child cover the number with a piece of torn construction paper. You can call out numbers in random order or call them out in order. My son enjoyed doing this activity for a few days.

LEARNING ABC'S

FRIDAY

Letter H Mystery Bag

Materials

- ☐ 4 Objects that Start with the Letter H (Ex. Paper Heart, Toy Horse, Hairbrush)
- ☐ 4 Objects that Start with a Different Letter (Ex. Truck, Water Bottle, Teddy Bear)
- ☐ Duffle Bag

Directions

Put all eight objects in to the duffle bag. Tell your toddler that there are surprises in your bag. Explain that some surprises start with the letter "H," and some surprises don't start with the letter "H." Ask him to reach into your bag and pull out one surprise. Ask him what the object is that he pulled out. Say the name of the object together with your child, and sound out the first letter of the object's name together. Ask your toddler if the object starts with "H." If it does start with an "H," put it in one pile, but if it doesn't start with the letter "H" put it in a different pile.

For example, if your toddler pulls out a truck. Ask him the name of the object. Next, you would say the word "truck" together. Sound out the first letter of truck to your toddler, "*t, t, truck.*" Now ask him if truck starts with "H." After he answers, put the truck in the "does not start with H" pile.

ALTERNATE ACTIVITY

Make Hedgehog Sandwiches

Materials

- ☐ Bread
- ☐ Knife or Heart Cookie Cutter
- ☐ Sandwich Filling (Cheese, Meat, PB&J, etc.)
- ☐ Pretzel Sticks
- ☐ 3 Chocolate Chips

Directions

Have your toddler assist you in making the sandwich—just make a regular sandwich. After you make your sandwich, have your toddler press the heart cookie cutter into the sandwich to cut the sandwich. If you don't have a heart cookie cutter, use a knife to cut the sandwich into a heart or triangle. Now have your toddler stick one chocolate chip at the pointy part of the heart; this is the nose. Next, ask your little one place the other two chocolate chips behind the nose for the hedgehog's eyes. After that, your child can stick pretzels all over the back of the hedgehog. (I broke the pretzels in half for my son to stick in the hedgehog.) Enjoy your tasty hedgehog!

The letter "I" has many pronunciations. Sometimes, it is pronounced "ee" like in "taxi." The letter "I" also has a short vowel sound of "ih." And a long vowel sound of "ai."

MONDAY

LOW PREP *Color an Iguana*

Materials

- ☐ Iguana Activity Page (Appendix R)
- ☐ Crayons

Directions

Show your toddler the *Iguana* activity page, and tell him the animal pictured on the page is an iguana. Tell him the word iguana starts with the letter "I," and that he will be learning about the letter "I" this week. Tell your little one what sound the letter "I" makes, "*i, i, iguana.*" Have him make the sound with you. Write the letter "I" on the *Iguana* activity page so he can see it. Then, your toddler can color the iguana however he chooses. When he is finished, hang the picture up somewhere so he can be proud of his work.

TUESDAY

LOW PREP *Make an I for Insect Picture*

Materials

- ☐ Insect Activity Page (Appendix S)
- ☐ Scissors
- ☐ Glue
- ☐ Construction Paper
- ☐ Crayons
- ☐ Pipe Cleaners (Optional)
- ☐ Hot Glue Gun (Optional)

Directions

Let your toddler color each part of the *Insect* activity page. Cut out the pieces from the *Insect* activity page. Ask your toddler to pick out a piece of construction paper on which to glue the insect. Assemble the insect, unglued, on the construction paper so your little one can see what the finished product should look like. Tell your toddler that the word insect starts with the letter "I." Next, tell him the sound, "*i, i, insect.*" Ask him to repeat it back to you. Ask your toddler to help rub glue on each piece of the insect, and press the pieces onto the construction paper. Assist your child as needed. We used pipe cleaners for the insects' antennas and legs, but this is not required. My son picked the colors, and I cut and glued them on with the hot glue gun. After the insect is complete, find a place to hang the picture so your little one can be proud of his work.

LEARNING ABC'S

WEDNESDAY

`LOW PREP` *Make an Igloo*

Materials

- ☐ Igloo Activity Page (Appendix T)
- ☐ Mini Marshmallows

Directions

Show your toddler the *Igloo* activity page, and tell him that it is an igloo. Tell him that the word igloo starts with the letter "I." Ask him if he knows what sound the letter "I" makes. Sound it out with him, "*i, i, igloo*." Next, tell your little one that he is going to build an igloo. Put a drop of glue in each block, and then your toddler can place a mini marshmallow on the glue. Explain that the marshmallows on the igloo cannot be eaten. It might be fun to count the marshmallows together when he is finished.

THURSDAY

`LOW PREP` *Make Insects in a Jar*

Materials

- ☐ Insect Activity Page (Appendix U)
- ☐ Washable Paint
- ☐ Marker

Directions

You will be helping your toddler finger paint insects in a jar. Ask your toddler what letter the word "insect" starts with, and then ask him if he knows what sound the letter "I" makes. Sound out the word insect with him, "*i, i, insect*." Your toddler can use the black paint to make three fingerprints in a row for an ant, and then draw legs and antennas on the ant with the marker. Next, use the yellow paint to make a dot in the jar for a bumblebee; draw strips, wings, and antennas on the yellow dot. Your little one can put a red paint dot in the jar for a ladybug. Draw black dots, legs and antennas on the ladybug with a marker. Now, ask your toddler to pick a color paint to make a butterfly. Put two fingerprint dots side by side. Draw the butterfly's body in between the dots and antennas with a marker. Encourage your child to add as many insects to the jar as he wishes.

FRIDAY

Letter I Mystery Bag

Materials

- ☐ 4 Objects that Start with the Letter I (Ex. Insect, Ivy, Ice)
- ☐ 4 Objects that Start with a Different Letter I(Ex. Car, Rattle, Paper)
- ☐ Duffle Bag

Directions

Put all eight objects in to the duffle bag. Tell your toddler that there are surprises in your bag. Explain that some surprises start with the letter "I", and some surprises don't start with the letter "I." Ask him to reach into your bag and pull out one surprise. Ask him what the object is that he pulled out. Say the name of the object together, and sound out the first letter of the object's name together. Ask your toddler if the object starts with the letter "I." If it does start with an "I," put it in one pile, but if it doesn't put it in a different pile.

For example, if your toddler pulls out ivy. Ask him the name of the object. Next, you would say "ivy" together. Sound out the first letter of the word ivy to your toddler, "*i, i, ivy*." Ask him if ivy starts with "I." After he answers, put the ivy in the "does start with I" pile.

ALTERNATE ACTIVITY

LOW PREP *Make Ice Cream in a Bag*

Materials

- ☐ ½ Cup of Half & Half
- ☐ ¼ Teaspoon of Vanilla Extract
- ☐ 1 Tablespoon of Sugar
- ☐ 1/3 Cup of Rock Salt
- ☐ For Chocolate Ice Cream: 2 Teaspoons of Cocoa Powder and ½ Teaspoon of Sugar
- ☐ 3 Cups of Ice
- ☐ 1 Gallon Size Freezer Bag
- ☐ 1 Sandwich Size Freezer Bag

Directions

Ask your child if he would like to make ice cream. Ask him if he can tell you the first letter in the word "ice cream." Next, ask him if he knows what sound the letter "I" makes. This will be a little tricky because he has been learning the short "I" sound all week, so if he makes the short "I" sound praise him, and explain to him that the letter "I" makes more than one sound. Make the short and long vowel sounds for "I," for example, "i, i, insect" and "i, i, ice cream." Have your toddler repeat the sounds with you. To make the ice cream, help your toddler pour the ice and salt into the gallon freezer bag. Then have your toddler mix the half & half, vanilla extract, and sugar (and cocoa if you are making chocolate ice cream) in the sandwich bag. Make sure you seal the sandwich bag tightly. Place the sandwich bag inside the gallon bag. Seal the gallon bag tightly, and let your child shake it for 5-10 minutes until it is frozen. The bag will become very cold, so it is helpful to wear gloves when shaking the bag. Scoop your ice cream into a bowl and enjoy!

LEARNING ABC'S

The letter "J" sound is formed by pushing the tongue against the upper ridge of the back of your top teeth, "juh."

MONDAY

LOW PREP *Make a J for Jellyfish Picture*

Materials

- ☐ Jellyfish Activity Page (Appendix V)
- ☐ Scissors
- ☐ Glue
- ☐ Construction Paper
- ☐ Crayons
- ☐ Pipe Cleaners (Optional)
- ☐ Hot Glue Gun (Optional)

Directions

Let your toddler color each part of the *Jellyfish* activity page. Cut out the pieces from the *Jellyfish* activity page. Ask your toddler to pick out a piece of construction paper on which to glue the jellyfish. Assemble the jellyfish, unglued, on the construction paper so your little one can see what the finished product should look like. Tell your toddler that jellyfish starts with the letter "J." Next, tell him the sound, "*j, j, jellyfish.*" Ask him to repeat it back to you. Ask your toddler to help rub glue on each piece of the jellyfish, and press the pieces onto the construction paper. Assist your child as needed. If you chose, you can use pipes cleaners for the legs. (My son picked the colors; I cut and glued them on with the hot glue gun.) After the jellyfish is complete, find a place to hang the picture so that your little one can be proud of his work.

─── **J** ───

TUESDAY

Play with Jello

Materials

- ☐ Disposable 9x13 Pan
- ☐ 4 packages of Jello
- ☐ Toys, Scoops, Cookie Cutters, etc.

Directions

Enlist your child to help you open and mix the 4 packages of Jello by simply following the instructions on the package. Afterwards, pour the mixture into a disposable 9x13 pan. Let the mixture firm up in the refrigerator. Tell your toddler that Jello starts with the letter "J." Make the sound for the letter, "*j, j, jello.*" Ask him to repeat the sound back to you. Once the Jello is firm, your toddler can have fun squishing it between his fingers, scooping it, rolling cars through it, or even eating it. (I do recommend this as an outside activity because it can get messy, but it's a lot of fun!)

WEDNESDAY

Make a Jellyfish in a Jar

Materials

- ☐ Clear Plastic Bag (Like a Produce Bag from the Grocery Store)
- ☐ Plastic Bottle
- ☐ Thread or String
- ☐ Water
- ☐ Scissors
- ☐ Blue Food Coloring

Directions

Ask your toddler if he would like to make his very own jellyfish. Ask him if he knows the first letter in the word jellyfish, and then ask him if he knows what sound the letter "J" makes. Sound it out together, *"j, j, jellyfish."* To make a jellyfish, cut the plastic bag so you have a flat rectangle, about a three by five inch rectangle. Gather the center of the rectangle so it forms a bubble about 1 ½ inches long. Tie your thread or string around the bubble, but not too tightly because you will fill the bubble with water. Cut strips to create jellyfish tentacles. Let your little one help you fill the bubble about half full of water. Next, let your toddler help you fill the plastic bottle all the way up with water. (I originally used a mason jar for this activity because that's all I had at the time, but you couldn't really see the jellyfish in the jar.) Let your toddler put some food coloring into the bottle, put the top on, and shake the bottle so that the food coloring spreads out. Now take the top off the bottle, and let your little one stuff the jellyfish in the bottle. Put the top back on, and enjoy watching the jellyfish float around.

Make Jelly

Materials

- ☐ 2 Cups of Sugar
- ☐ 1 Pound of Strawberries
- ☐ Juice from Half a Lemon
- ☐ Small Plate
- ☐ Jar for the Jelly

Directions

Tell your toddler that he will get to make jelly today. Ask your toddler if he knows the first letter in the word "jelly," and then ask him what sound the letter "J" makes. Sound it out with him, *"j, j, jelly."* (We made strawberry jelly, but you could substitute another fruit.)

First, place your plate in the freezer. Next, have your toddler help you wash the strawberries. As your toddler washes the strawberries, take the stems off of the strawberries. Place the strawberries in a pot and mash them with a potato masher. This is a fun task for your toddler to do, but it can get out of hand, so be careful. Add in the lemon juice and mix together. Ask your toddler to add the sugar into the pot. Turn the heat to medium low, and continue to stir. Raise the heat to high so that the jelly is boiling. Boil for 10 minutes, but keep stirring as it is boiling. After the 10 minutes, take the plate out of the freezer and pour about one teaspoon on the plate, draw a line through the middle of the jelly. If the line remains clear the jelly is done, but if it's still runny, cook for five more minutes and retest it. Once it's finished, take the jelly off the heat, let it cool, and put it in a jar. Now your child and you can enjoy a peanut butter and jelly sandwich with your homemade jelly.

THURSDAY

LEARNING ABC'S

FRIDAY

Letter J Mystery Bag

Materials

- ☐ 4 Objects that Start with the Letter J (Ex. Juice Box, Jaguar, Jar)
- ☐ 4 Objects that Start with a Different Letter (Ex. Hammer, Cup, Towel)
- ☐ Duffle Bag

Directions

Put all eight objects in to the duffle bag. Tell your toddler that there are surprises in your bag. Explain that some surprises start with the letter "J," and some surprises don't start with the letter "J." Ask him to reach into your bag and pull out one surprise. Ask him what the object is that he pulled out. Say the name of the object together, and sound out the first letter of the object's name together. Ask your toddler if the object starts with "J." If it does start with a "J," then put it in one pile, but if it doesn't put it in a different pile.

For example, if your toddler pulls out a hammer. Ask him the name of the object. Next, you would say "hammer" together. Sound out the first letter of the word hammer to your toddler, "*h, h, hammer*." Now ask him if the word hammer starts with "J." After he answers, put the hammer in the "does not start with J" pile.

 # ALTERNATE ACTIVITY

LOW PREP *Jumping J's*

Materials

- ☐ Paper
- ☐ Markers
- ☐ Tape

Directions

Write the letter "J" on 10 pieces of paper. Write five uppercase "J's" and five lowercase "j's." Write them in different colors too. Now tape them on the floor all over your house. (We used the living room and kitchen for our game.) Ask your toddler if he would like to play a game. Tell him that this is a jumping game. Tell him that the word "jumping" starts with the letter "J." Ask your little one if he knows what sound the letter "J" makes. Help him sound it out, "*j, j, jumping*." Tell him that you will ask him to find a certain color uppercase "J" or lowercase "j," and he will need to jump to it. Do an example with him. Ask him if he can find the uppercase, red "J." When he spots it, you will both jump to it.

To create the letter "K" sound, air is briefly prevented from leaving the throat when the back of the tongue presses against the palate at the back of the mouth, "kk."

MONDAY

Make a Kite

Materials

- ☐ Half a Poster Board
- ☐ Scissors
- ☐ Paint, Glitter, Crayons, Tissue Paper, etc.
- ☐ 5 Craft Sticks
- ☐ 4 Feet of String
- ☐ Hot Glue Gun

Directions

Tell your toddler that he will be learning about the letter "K" this week. Tell him the sound of the letter "K," "k, k, kite." Tell your toddler that he will get to make a kite today. You will need to cut your half size poster board into a diamond. Then let your little one decorate it. Once his kite is beautiful, turn the kite over and hot glue four craft sticks onto the kite—you will want it to look like a lowercase "t". You can also hot glue one end of the string to the bottom of the back of the kite. Now wrap the other end of the string around your fifth craft stick. If there is a nice breeze outside, you and your child one can try to fly the kite.

(Our kites did not fly very well outside, but they were fun to make.)

TUESDAY

LOW PREP ### Kick the Ball

Materials

- ☐ Ball
- ☐ Tape

Directions

Using tape, form the letter "K" and tape it onto a ball. Ask your toddler what letter is on the ball. Tell him the sound that the letter "K" makes, "k, k, kick." Have him repeat it back to you. Tell him that he will be kicking the letter "K." This is a good outside activity.

LEARNING ABC'S

WEDNESDAY

LOW PREP *Make a K for Kangaroo Picture*

Materials

- ☐ Kangaroo Activity Page (Appendix W)
- ☐ Scissors
- ☐ Glue Stick
- ☐ Construction Paper
- ☐ Crayons

Directions

Let your toddler color each part of the *Kangaroo* activity page. Cut out the pieces from the *Kangaroo* activity page. Ask your toddler to pick out a piece of construction paper on which to glue the kangaroo. Assemble the kangaroo, unglued, on the construction paper so your little one can see what the finished product should look like. Tell your toddler that kangaroo starts with the letter "K." Next tell him the sound, "*k, k, kangaroo.*" Ask him to repeat it back to you. Ask your toddler to help rub glue on each piece of the kangaroo, and press the pieces onto the construction paper. Assist your child as needed. After the kangaroo is complete, find a place to hang the picture so your little one can be proud of his work.

THURSDAY

LOW PREP *Make a Key*

Materials

- ☐ Key Activity Page (Appendix X)
- ☐ Scissors
- ☐ Glue
- ☐ Aluminum Foil

Directions

Prepare for this activity by cutting up or tearing strips of aluminum foil.

Ask your toddler if he would like to make a key. Show him the *Key* activity page to help peak his interest. Ask him if he knows what letter the word key starts with, and then ask if he knows what sound the letter "K" makes. Make the sound with him, "*k, k, key.*" Now flip your *Key* activity page over. The key is now facing down. Ask your toddler to rub glue on the page. Depending on how the glue dries, you may need to work in sections on the paper. After the glue is on the paper, have your toddler add pieces of aluminum foil all over the paper to make a collage. Make sure it is pressed down flat. When the paper is covered in foil, you can flip it over and cut out the key for your toddler.

FRIDAY

Letter K Mystery Bag

Materials

- ☐ 4 Objects that Start with the Letter K (Ex. Koala, Kangaroo, Key)
- ☐ 4 Objects that Start with a Different Letter (Ex. Ball, Bowl, Leaf)
- ☐ Duffle Bag

Directions

Put all eight objects in to the duffle bag. Tell your toddler that there are surprises in your bag. Explain that some surprises start with the letter "K," and some surprises don't start with the letter "K." Ask him to reach into your bag and pull out one surprise. Ask him what the object is that he pulled out. Say the name of the object together, and sound out the first letter of the object's name together. Ask your toddler if the object starts with the letter "K." If the word starts with a "K," put it in one pile, but if it doesn't, put it in a different pile.

For example, if your toddler pulls out a key. Ask him the name of the object. Next, say the word "key" together. Sound out the first letter of key to your toddler, "*k, k, key*." Now ask him if the word key starts with "K." After he answers, put the key in the "does start with K" pile.

 # ALTERNATE ACTIVITY

LOW PREP *Kitten Knitting*

Materials

- ☐ Kitten Activity Page (Appendix Y)
- ☐ Crayon

Directions

Using the *Kitten* activity page, show your toddler that this kitten wants to knit, but is having a really hard time finding the yarn. Ask your toddler if he can help the kitten find the yarn. Ask him if he knows the first letter in the word "kitten." Ask him if he knows what sound the letter "K" makes. Sound it out together, "*k, k, kitten*." Now use your finger to show your toddler that he will trace the line to find each color yarn. Let him pick out a crayon to use to trace the lines. If this is his first time tracing, you might want to guide his hand on the first line.

MONDAY

To make the letter "L" sound place the tip of your tongue against the ridge behind your upper front teeth, let air flow around the tongue and turn on your voice to form the "ll" sound.

LOW PREP *Make an L for Ladybug Picture*

Materials

- ☐ Ladybug Activity Page (Appendix Z)
- ☐ Scissors
- ☐ Glue Stick
- ☐ Construction Paper
- ☐ Crayons
- ☐ Black Paint (Optional)

Directions

Let your toddler color each part of the *Ladybug* activity page. (We used black paint for the dots; you can use paint or crayons.) Cut out the pieces from the *Ladybug* activity page. Ask your toddler to pick out a piece of construction paper on which to glue the ladybug. Assemble the ladybug, unglued, on the construction paper so that your little one can see what the finished product should look like. Tell your toddler that the word ladybug starts with the letter "L." Next, tell him the sound, "*l, l, ladybug.*" Ask him to repeat it back to you. Ask your toddler to help rub glue on each piece of the ladybug, and press the pieces onto the construction paper. Assist your child as needed. When the ladybug is glued down you can have your toddler add black dots to the ladybug wings by dipping his finger in the paint and just pressing his finger on the wing a few times. After the ladybug is dry, find a place to hang the picture so that your little one can be proud of his work.

LOW PREP *Make Lemonade*

Materials

- ☐ 1 Cup of Sugar
- ☐ 1 Cup of Water (for the Syrup)
- ☐ 1 Cup of Lemon Juice (4-6 Lemons)
- ☐ 2-3 Cups of Cold Water (to Dilute)
- ☐ Spoon
- ☐ Saucepan
- ☐ Pitcher
- ☐ Knife

TUESDAY

Directions

Ask your little one if he would like to help you make some lemonade. Tell your toddler that lemonade starts with the letter "L." Make the sound for him, "*l, l, lemonade.*" Ask him to repeat it back to you.

First, you will need to juice your lemons. You can go ahead and juice them into your pitcher. It helps if you roll the lemons around before you cut them and squeeze the juice out. I had my son roll the lemons around the counter while I cut and squeezed one lemon. After I squeezed the lemons, I let him squeeze the juice out of the lemons too. Once you have your lemons juiced, make your syrup by placing one cup of water and sugar into a saucepan, and bring to a simmer. Make sure you stir it so the sugar dissolves, and then remove from the heat. Pour the syrup into your pitcher with the lemon juice. Add two to three cups of cold water, and let your toddler stir. Add more water to dilute the lemonade if needed, or more lemon juice if it's too sweet. Sit down and enjoy a cup of lemonade with your little one!

   LEARNING ABC'S

WEDNESDAY

Make a Lion Mask
Materials

- ☐ 1 Paper Plate
- ☐ Glue
- ☐ Brown, Yellow and Orange Construction Paper
- ☐ 1 Craft Stick
- ☐ Scissors
- ☐ Tape

Directions

Ask your toddler if he would like to be a lion today. Tell your toddler that the word lion starts with the letter "L." Ask him if he knows what sound the letter "L" makes. Next, sound it out together with your child, "*l, l, lion.*"

Cut the center of the paper plate out so you toddler's face will fit in the center of the plate. Cut some orange and yellow one by three inch strips from the construction paper for the lion's mane. Cut out two half circles from the brown construction paper for the lion's ears. Now your toddler can glue the orange and yellow strips of paper all over the paper plate. It makes a good mane if some of the strips are hanging off the plate, but your child should feel free to follow his creative tastes. After he finishes the mane, have him glue the ears on the top edge of the paper plate; it's okay if it's on top of the mane. Now flip the lion's mane over and tape the craft stick to the bottom of the paper plate so your toddler is able to hold the mask up to his face.

Make a Lava Lamp
Materials

- ☐ An Empty Water Bottle
- ☐ Food Coloring
- ☐ Vegetable Oil
- ☐ Water
- ☐ Alka Seltzer
- ☐ Funnel

Directions

This activity was my son's all time favorite activity from the whole unit. He would show his "laba lamp" to everyone that came to our house or ask to FaceTime family to show them.

Ask your toddler if he would like to make a lava lamp. Ask him if he knows the first letter in the word "lava." Ask him if he knows what sound the letter "L" makes. Sound it out together with your child, "*l, l, lava*" and '*l, l, lamp.*" Place the funnel in the water bottle so your toddler can help you pour in the vegetable oil. Fill the water bottle two-thirds full with vegetable oil. Next, fill the rest of the water bottle with water leaving an inch at the top. Now your toddler can add food coloring to the bottle. Allow him to pick the color. Break your alka seltzer tablet into three or four pieces and hand your toddler one piece at a time to drop into the bottle. Watch his face light up as the mixture begins to bubble.

THURSDAY

LEARNING ABC'S

FRIDAY

Letter L Mystery Bag

Materials

- ☐ 4 Objects that Start with the Letter L (Ex. Lion, Lemon, Level)
- ☐ 4 Objects that Start with a Different Letter (Ex. Toothpaste, Granola Bar, Block)
- ☐ Duffle Bag

Directions

Put all eight objects in to the duffle bag. Tell your toddler that there are surprises in your bag. Explain that some surprises start with the letter "L," and some surprises don't start with the letter "L." Ask him to reach into your bag and pull out one surprise. Ask him the name of the object he pulled out. Say the name of the object together with your child, and sound out the first letter of the object's name together. Ask your toddler if the object starts with "L." If it starts with the letter "L," put it in one pile, but if it does not start with the letter "L," put it in a different pile.

For example, if your toddler pulls out a lemon. Ask him the name of the object. Next, you would say the word "lemon" together. Sound out the first letter of lemon to your toddler, "l, l, lemon." Now ask him if lemon starts with the letter "L." After he answers, put the lemon in the "does start with L" pile.

ALTERNATE ACTIVITY

Lace the Letter L

Materials

- ☐ Poster Board
- ☐ Scissors
- ☐ Single Hole Puncher
- ☐ String
- ☐ Pipe Cleaner or Tape

Directions

Cut out a big, uppercase letter "L" from your poster board—about 18 inches tall. Using a hole puncher, punch holes around the edges of the letter "L" every two inches. Outline the edge of the letter "L" with your string and add six more inches before you cut it. Cut the string, and tie one end around one of your holes on the letter "L." Take the other end of the string and either tape the end so the string doesn't fray or tie a small piece of pipe cleaner around the end like a sewing needle. (I chose to do the pipe cleaner so that it would be an easier tool for my son to manipulate as he was lacing the letter "L.")

Once you have the letter "L" set up, ask your toddler if he would like to lace the letter "L." Ask him if he knows the first letter in the word "lace." Ask him if he knows what sound the letter "L" makes. Make the sound together with your child, "l, l, lace." Now show him how he will take the string and lace it through the hole. Have him lace the letter "L" around the edge, or he can lace it whatever way he chooses.

   LEARNING ABC'S

The letter "M" sound is made by pressing both lips together while making the "mm" sound with your vocal cords.

MONDAY

LOW PREP *Magic Milk*

Materials

- ☐ Milk
- ☐ Food Coloring
- ☐ Dish Soap
- ☐ Small Bowl
- ☐ Toothpick
- ☐ Pie Pan or Shallow Bowl

Directions

Ask your toddler if he knows that milk is magic. Tell him that you can show him how milk is magic. First, pour the milk into your pan. You just need to cover the bottom of the pan. Next, ask your toddler to pick out four colors of food coloring. Put a few drops of each food coloring around the milk. Pour some dish soap into a small bowl. Now for the magic part, dip a toothpick into the dish soap, and then dip it into the food coloring. The food coloring should move away from the toothpick. Ask your toddler if he wants to try the magic trick. Tell him to dip the toothpick into the soap, and then into one of the colors. He can do this as many times as he would like. He can also draw in the milk with the toothpick. As he is performing his magic tell him that magic and milk start with the letter "M." Tell him the sound of the letter "M," "*m, m, magic*" and "*m, m, milk*." Have him repeat it to you.

TUESDAY

LOW PREP *Make an M for Mouse Picture*

Materials

- ☐ Mouse Activity Page (Appendix AA)
- ☐ Scissors
- ☐ Glue Stick
- ☐ Construction Paper
- ☐ Crayons

Directions

Let your toddler color each part of the *Mouse* activity page. Cut out the pieces from the *Mouse* activity page. Ask your toddler to pick out a piece of construction paper on which to glue the mouse. Assemble the mouse, unglued, on the construction paper so your little one can see what the finished product should look like. Tell your toddler that mouse starts with the letter "M." Next, tell him the sound, "*m, m, mouse*." Ask him to repeat it back to you. Ask your toddler to help rub glue on each piece of the mouse, and press the pieces onto the construction paper. Assist your child as needed. After the mouse is complete, find a place to hang the picture so your little one can be proud of his work.

WEDNESDAY

LOW PREP M&M Sorting

Materials

- ☐ M&M Activity Page (Appendix AB)
- ☐ M&M's

Directions

Ask your toddler if he would like to sort M&M's today. Open the bag of M&M's, and show him all of the different colors. Tell him that in this activity he will pick up an M&M, say the color of the M&M, and then place it on the chart in the correct column. Show him how to do it two times, and then let him do it. (My son was more interested in eating the M&M's than doing the activity, but he at least said the color he was eating.) When your little one is finished sorting the M&M's ask him which color has the most M&M's and which color has the least number of M&M's. You can also count the number in each group. Now enjoy a chocolaty treat!

LOW PREP Read *If You Give a Moose a Muffin* and Make Muffins

THURSDAY

Materials

- ☐ If You Give a Moose a Muffin
- ☐ Muffin Mix-Ingredients from Box
- ☐ Muffin Pan
- ☐ Cupcake Liners
- ☐ Bowl
- ☐ Spoon

Directions

Buy the book *If You Give a Moose a Muffin* or check it out from the library. Some toddlers probably enjoy holding the book and flipping through the pages as you read, but if that is not an option, you can listen to someone read the story online. After you read the story together tell your little one that moose starts with the letter "M" and muffin starts with the letter "M." Sound out both words for him, "*m, m, moose*" and "*m, m, muffin*." Next, make muffins together. Follow the directions from the box. Let you toddler assist you by pouring the ingredients into the bowl, stirring, and placing the cupcake liners in the muffin pan. As you are baking, ask your toddler if he knows the first letter in the word muffin, and ask him to pronounce the sound of the letter "M." Enjoy your muffins!

FRIDAY

Letter M Mystery Bag

Materials

- ☐ 4 Objects that Start with the Letter M (Ex. Movie, Macaroni, Maracas)
- ☐ 4 Objects that Start with a Different Letter (Ex. Crayon, Washcloth, Golf Ball)
- ☐ Duffle Bag

Directions

Put all eight objects in to the duffle bag. Tell your toddler that there are surprises in your bag. Explain that some surprises start with the letter "M," and some surprises don't start with the letter "M." Ask him to reach into your bag and pull out one surprise. Ask him the name of the object he pulled out. Say the name of the object together, and sound out the first letter of the object's name together. Ask your toddler if the object starts with "M." If it does start with an "M," put it in one pile, but if it doesn't start with the letter "M" put it in a different pile.

For example, if your toddler pulls out a washcloth. Ask him the name of the object. Next, you would say "washcloth" together with your child. Sound out the first letter of washcloth to your toddler, "w, w, washcloth." Now ask him if the word washcloth starts with the letter "M." After he answers, put the washcloth in the "does not start with M" pile.

ALTERNATE ACTIVITY

LOW PREP *Make Maracas*

Materials

- ☐ Rice
- ☐ Plastic Eggs
- ☐ 2 Plastic Spoons
- ☐ Tape

Directions

Show your toddler a video of someone playing maracas and point out the maracas. Tell your toddler that maraca starts with the letter "M." Sound it out together, "m, m, maraca." Ask your toddler if he would like to make his very own maraca. Let your little one put some rice in the plastic egg. Close the plastic egg. Now lay one spoon flat on the table, have your toddler place the plastic egg in the spoon, and place the other spoon on top of the plastic egg. Now, wrap tape around the spoons and egg. Wrap tape around the spoon handles also. Enjoy the sweet music your toddler will make all day!

The letter "N" sound is made by pressing the tip of the tongue against the tooth ridge. Air passes out through the nose as the "nn" sound is made.

MONDAY

LOW PREP *Make a Necklace*

Materials

☐ String
☐ Fruit Loops, Beads, Noodles

Directions

Tell your toddler that he will be learning about the letter "N" this week, and today he will get to make a necklace. Tell him that necklace starts with the letter "N." Sound out the letter "N." with him, "*n, n, necklace.*" Cut some string that can fit around his neck with a little extra slack. (We used things we had around the house like Fruit Loops and noodles for our necklace beads.) Tie a bead around one end of the necklace to prevent all of the beads from falling off. Now let your toddler have fun adding other beads to his necklace. If he uses Fruit Loops to make his necklace, then he can enjoy a snack as he wears his necklace. When he is finished, tie the ends together and place it around your toddler's neck. (Parents please use caution by using a light weight string that will break easily if a brother or friend chooses to pull on the necklace while your child is wearing it.)

TUESDAY

Play in Noodles

Materials

☐ Large Pot
☐ Water
☐ 4 Packs of Spaghetti Noodles
☐ 4 Colors of Food Coloring
☐ Vegetable Oil (Optional)
☐ Large Plastic Container

Directions

This is a silly and fun activity, but it does take some preparation. You will need to cook each pack of spaghetti noodles in a large pot of water one at a time. Pick a color of food coloring to add to each batch. Add a tablespoon of vegetable oil to each batch as it cooks to prevent the noodles from sticking together. After you cook one batch of noodles, drain them, and pour them into the plastic container. Then you can work on the next batch of noodles. Each batch should be the color of food coloring that you added to the pot. After you have cooked all of the noodles and they have cooled, invite your toddler to play in the noodles. (Our plastic container was big enough that it enabled my son to climb in and bathe in the noodles. He had a lot of fun putting them on his head and squishing the noodles with his toes.) As your little one is playing in the noodles tell him that noodles start with the letter "N." Sound it out with him, "*n, n, noodles.*" Have him repeat the sound to you.

WEDNESDAY

LOW PREP *Make an N for Night Picture*

Materials

- ☐ Night Activity Page (Appendix AC)
- ☐ Scissors
- ☐ Glue Stick
- ☐ Construction Paper
- ☐ Crayons
- ☐ Yellow Paint (Optional)

Directions

Let your toddler color each part of the *Night* activity page. Cut out the pieces from the *Night* activity page. Ask your toddler to pick out a black piece of construction paper on which to glue the moon and stars. Assemble the night picture, unglued, on the construction paper so your little one can see what the finished product should look like. Tell your toddler that night starts with the letter "N." Next, tell him the sound, "*n, n, night.*" Ask him to repeat it back to you. Ask your toddler to help rub glue on each piece of the night picture, and press the pieces onto the construction paper. Assist your child as needed. When the night picture is glued down, ask your toddler to use his finger and the yellow washable paint to make stars all over the night picture. After the night picture is dry, find a place to hang the picture so your little one can be proud of his work.

Make Rice Krispy Treat Nests

THURSDAY

Materials

- ☐ 3 Tablespoons of Butter
- ☐ 10oz Bag of Marshmallows
- ☐ 6 Cups of Rice Krispies
- ☐ Edible Grass or Green Frosting
- ☐ Robins Egg Candy or Peanut M&M's
- ☐ Large Pot
- ☐ Muffin Pan
- ☐ Cooking Spray
- ☐ Spoon

Directions

Ask your little one if he would like to help you make some bird's nests that can be eaten. Ask him if he knows the first letter in the word "nest." Ask him if he knows what sound the letter "N" makes. Make the sound together with your child, "*n, n, nest.*" Have your toddler put the butter in the pot. Let the butter begin to melt, and then your little one can pour in the marshmallows. Continue to stir the mixture until it is all melted. Pour the rice krispies into the marshmallow mixture. Stir it all together. Spray the muffin pan with cooking spray. Scoop the rice krispy mixture into the muffin pan and form nests. Your toddler can help form the nests by pressing the rice krispy mixture against the walls on the muffin cup. Let the rice krispy treats cool in the muffin pan. Add your edible grass or green frosting and eggs. (We chose to just add eggs since this treat already has a lot of sugar.) Enjoy your nests!

LEARNING ABC'S

FRIDAY

Letter N Mystery Bag

Materials

- ☐ 4 Objects that Start with the Letter N (Ex. Noodle, Necklace, Number)
- ☐ 4 Objects that Start with a Different Letter (Ex. Truck, Strawberry, Popsicle Stick)
- ☐ Duffle Bag

Directions

Put all eight objects in to the duffle bag. Tell your toddler that there are surprises in your bag. Explain that some surprises start with the letter "N," and some surprises don't start with the letter "N." Ask him to reach into your bag and pull out one surprise. Ask him what the object is that he pulled out. Say the name of the object together, and sound out the first letter of the object's name together. Ask your toddler if the object starts with the letter "N." If it does start with an "N," then put it in one pile, but if it doesn't start with the letter "N," put it in a different pile.

For example, if your toddler pulls out a popsicle stick. Ask him the name of the object. Next, you would say "popsicle stick" together with your child. Sound out the first letter of popsicle stick to your toddler, "*p, p, popsicle stick.*" Now ask him if popsicle stick starts with the letter "N." After he answers, put the popsicle stick in the "does not start with N" pile.

ALTERNATE ACTIVITY

LOW PREP *Number Activity*

Materials

- ☐ Index Cards
- ☐ Marker
- ☐ Dried Noodles

Directions

Use the marker to write a number on each index card. Number the cards 1 through 10. Ask your toddler if he wants to count with noodles. Lay the index cards in front of him, in order. Count the cards together. Tell your toddler that the word "number" starts with the letter "N." Ask your little one if he knows what sound the letter "N" makes. Sound it out together with your child, "*n, n, number.*" Now give him some dried noodles, and explain to him that he should place the correct number of noodles on each card. You can also ask your toddler to tell you the first letter in the word noodle.

I ask my son the number on the card, and then I ask him how many noodles we need (the same number). I then hand him that many noodles for him to place on the card. Once the noodles are on the card we count the noodles.

   LEARNING ABC'S

The letter "O" has two sounds. A short sound, "awe" and a long sound, "oh." These activities focus on using the short "O" sound.

MONDAY

LOW PREP *Make an O for Ostrich Picture*

Materials

- ☐ Ostrich Activity Page (Appendix AD)
- ☐ Scissors
- ☐ Glue Stick
- ☐ Construction Paper
- ☐ Crayons

Directions

Let your toddler color each part of the *Ostrich* activity page. Cut out the pieces from the *Ostrich* activity page. Ask your toddler to pick out a piece of construction paper on which to glue the ostrich. Assemble the ostrich, unglued, on the construction paper so your little one can see what the finished product should look like. Tell your toddler that ostrich starts with the letter "O." Next, tell him the sound, "*o, o, ostrich.*" Ask him to repeat it back to you. Ask your toddler to help rub glue on each piece of the ostrich, and press the pieces onto the construction paper. Assist your child as needed. After the ostrich is complete, find a place to hang the picture so that your little one can be proud of his work.

TUESDAY

LOW PREP *Octopus Math*

Materials

- ☐ Octopus Activity Page (Appendix AE)
- ☐ Stickers

Directions

Show your little one the picture of the octopus. Explain that it has eight legs. Count the legs together. Tell your little one that octopus starts with the letter "O." Tell him the sound, "*o, o, octopus.*" Ask him to repeat the sound to you. Now tell your toddler that he will get to put stickers on the octopus's legs. He will put the correct number of stickers to match the labeled legs. (We used the circle label stickers, but you can use any type of sticker.)

I like to ask my son what number is on the leg, and then I ask him how many stickers I need for that leg (the same number). Next, I hand him the correct number of stickers.

LEARNING ABC'S

WEDNESDAY

Make Waffle Owls

Materials

- ☐ Waffle
- ☐ Banana
- ☐ Apple
- ☐ Blueberries or Chocolate Chips
- ☐ Peanut Butter or Cream Cheese

Directions

Ask your toddler if he wants to help you make an owl. Tell him the word "owl" starts with the letter "O." Ask him if he knows what sound the letter "O" makes. Sound it out together, "o, o, owl." Gather all of your ingredients, and assemble your owl. (I used frozen waffles because I don't have a waffle maker, but you are welcome to make a waffle from scratch.)

Heat up your waffle, and slice your banana into round slices. You will need two banana slices for the eyes. Ask your toddler to place the banana slices on the waffle close to the edge. Now put a dab of peanut butter or cream cheese in the center of the banana slices. Ask your little one to place a blueberry or chocolate chip on top of the peanut butter or cream cheese. These are your owl's eyes. Slice your apple into half circle shaped slivers. You will need two slivers for the wings and half a sliver for the beak. Place a dab of peanut butter or cream cheese to the sides of the banana slices. Ask your toddler to place an apple sliver on each dab—the round edge should be facing away from the banana slices. These are your owl's wings. Now slice an apple sliver in half. Place a dab of peanut butter or cream cheese under the owl's eyes. Ask your toddler to place the half apple sliver on the dab. This is your owl's beak. Ta da—you have a cute owl to eat!

THURSDAY

`LOW PREP` O Stamping

Materials

- ☐ Toilet Paper Tube(s)
- ☐ Paint
- ☐ Paper Plate
- ☐ Construction Paper

Directions

Ask your toddler if he would like to stamp. Tell him that he will get to make a picture with a bunch of "O's" on it. Let him pick out a piece of construction paper. Let him pick out one or more color paints. (I recommend having a toilet paper tube for each color of paint so the paint doesn't get mixed together.) Pour the paint on the paper plate and place a toilet paper tube in each color. Tell your toddler that he can use the tubes to stamp 'O's" onto the paper. Show him the "O's" he makes as he is painting.

FRIDAY

Letter O Mystery Bag

Materials

- ☐ 4 Objects that Start with the Letter O (Ex. Ostrich, Owl, Orange)
- ☐ 4 Objects that Start with a Different Letter (Ex. Candle, Screwdriver, Grape)
- ☐ Duffle Bag

Directions

Put all eight objects in to the duffle bag. Tell your toddler that there are surprises in your bag. Explain that some surprises start with the letter "O," and some surprises don't start with the letter "O." Ask him to reach into your bag and pull out one surprise. Ask him what the object is that he pulled out. Say the name of the object together, and sound out the first letter of the object's name together. Ask your toddler if the object starts with the letter "O." If it does start with an "O," put it in one pile, but if it doesn't start with the letter "O," put it in a different pile.

For example, if your toddler pulls out an owl ask him the name of the object. Next, you would say "owl" together with your child. Sound out the first letter of owl to your toddler, "o, o, owl." Now ask him if owl starts with the letter "O." After he answers, put the owl in the "does start with O" pile.

 # ALTERNATE ACTIVITY

Otter Puppet

Materials

- ☐ Otter Activity Page (Appendix AF)
- ☐ Brown Paper Lunch Bag
- ☐ Glue
- ☐ Crayons

Directions

Ask your little one if he would like to make an otter puppet today. Ask him if he knows the first letter in the word "otter." Ask him if he knows what sound the letter "O" makes. Make the sound together, "o, o, otter."

Let your toddler color each part of the *Otter* activity page. Cut out the patterns from the *Otter* activity page. Assemble the otter, unglued, to the paper bag so your toddler can see what the otter is supposed to look like when it's complete. Your paper bag should be laying flat with the open end closest to your toddler. The folded portion of the bag should be face up. The ears will go in the top corners of the folded portion of the bag. The eyes and nose will be on the folded flap of the bag. The otter's hands will go on the sides of the bag. The otter's feet will be on the bottom corners of the bag. The tail will go on the back of the bag so that it hangs down in between the otter's feet. Now ask your toddler to rub glue on each piece of the otter, and push it down onto the paper bag. After each piece is glued down, your toddler can play with his new puppet.

 **LEARNING ABC'S**

To make the letter "P" sound press both lips together and then release air in an explosive manner, "puh."

MONDAY

LOW PREP *Make Pizza*

Materials

- ☐ Pizza Crust
- ☐ Pizza Sauce
- ☐ Mozzarella
- ☐ Pizza Toppings
- ☐ Pizza Pan

Directions

Ask your little one if he wants to help you make some pizza. Tell him that pizza starts with the letter "P," and he will be learning about the letter "P" this week. Sound out the letter for him, "*p, p, pizza.*" Prepare your pizza crust following the directions on the "box." (I typically purchase pizza crust mix that only requires adding hot water to the mix. It is simple and easy.)

After the crust is mixed, ask your child to help you spread it out on the pan. Now let your little one scoop some pizza sauce onto the pizza crust and spread it around. Next, let him add the mozzarella cheese covering the pizza sauce. Add any toppings that you would like to have on your pizza. Cook the pizza according to the directions on the pizza crust package. Enjoy your little one's tasty creation after it cools.

TUESDAY

LOW PREP *Make a P for Penguin Picture*

Materials

- ☐ Penguin Activity Page (Appendix AG)
- ☐ Scissors
- ☐ Glue Stick
- ☐ Construction Paper
- ☐ Crayons

Directions

Let your toddler color each part of the *Penguin* activity page. Cut out the pieces from the *Penguin* activity page. Ask your toddler to pick out a piece of construction paper on which to glue the penguin. Assemble the penguin, unglued, on the construction paper so that your little one can see what the finished product should look like when it is complete. Tell your toddler that penguin starts with the letter "P." Next, tell him the sound, "*p, p, penguin.*" Ask him to repeat it back to you. Ask your toddler to help rub glue on each piece of the penguin, and press the pieces onto the construction paper. Assist your child as needed.

WEDNESDAY

Make Pom Pom Shooters

Materials

☐ Solo Cups
☐ Scissors
☐ Balloons
☐ Tape
☐ Pom Poms

Directions

Ask your toddler if he would like to make a Pom Pom Shooter. Tell your toddler that "Pom Pom" starts with the letter "P." Ask your toddler if he knows what sound the letter "P" makes. Sound it out with him, "*p, p, Pom Pom.*" To assemble the Pom Pom Shooter you will need to cut off the bottom of the cup. Now, tie a knot in the end of the balloon—like you just blew it up. Next, cut about ½ inch of the balloon top off—the end that does not have a knot. Place the cup down on a flat surface with the cut off end facing up. Stretch the balloon over the cup so it is covering the opening of the cup, and release the balloon. Place tape on the edges of the balloon so it will not pop off. Now you can place a Pom Pom inside the cup, pull the balloon knot down, let it go, and watch the Pom Pom fly! See whose Pom Pom can fly further.

Paint with Popcorn

Materials

☐ Popcorn
☐ Paper
☐ Paint
☐ Paper Plate

Directions

You will need to pop a bag of popcorn for this activity. Ask your toddler if he would like to paint a picture using popcorn. Ask your toddler if he knows the first letter in the word "popcorn." Ask him if he knows what sound the letter "P" makes. Sound it out with him, "*p, p, popcorn.*" Allow your child to pick a few colors of paint that he would like to use. Put the paint onto the paper plate so your toddler can dip the popcorn into the paint. Show him how he can dip the popcorn into the paint and then spread the paint on the paper. You might have to replace the pieces of popcorn a few times because they do get soggy. Let your little one make a beautiful creation.

THURSDAY

LEARNING ABC'S

FRIDAY

Letter P Mystery Bag

Materials

- ☐ 4 Objects that Start with the Letter P (Ex. Peach, Pom Pom, Pen)
- ☐ 4 Objects that Start with a Different Letter (Ex. Blanket, Truck, Zipper)
- ☐ Duffle Bag

Directions

Put all eight objects in to the duffle bag. Tell your toddler that there are surprises in your bag. Explain that some surprises start with the letter "P," and some surprises don't start with the letter "P." Ask him to reach into your bag and pull out one surprise. Ask him what the object is that he pulled out. Say the name of the object together, and sound out the first letter of the object's name together. Ask your toddler if the object starts with "P." If it does start with a "P," put it in one pile, but if it doesn't start with the letter "P," put it in a different pile.

For example, if your toddler pulls out a blanket. Ask him the name of the object. Next, you would say "blanket" together. Sound out the first letter of blanket to your toddler, "*b, b, blanket.*" Now ask him if blanket starts with the letter "P." After he answers, put the blanket in the "does not start with P" pile.

ALTERNATE ACTIVITY

LOW PREP *Find the Letter on the Pumpkin*

Materials

- ☐ Pumpkin Activity Page (Appendix AH)
- ☐ Single Hole Puncher

Directions

Ask your toddler if he would like to punch holes in a pumpkin. Tell your toddler that pumpkin starts with the letter "P." Ask him if he knows what sound the letter "P" makes. Sound it out together with your child, "*p, p, pumpkin.*" Now show your toddler the *Pumpkin* activity page with all of the letters on it. Tell him that you will ask him to find a letter on the pumpkin, and when he finds the letter, he will punch a hole on it. You may have to help your child squeeze the hole puncher. Call out the letters in any order you wish.

The letter "Q" makes a sound that combines the "K" and "W" sound together to sound like this, "kwa."

MONDAY

LOW PREP *Trace Letters with a Q-Tip*

Materials

- ☐ Whiteboard
- ☐ Dry Erase Markers
- ☐ Q-Tips

Directions

Ask your little one if he would like to use a Q-tip to trace letters. Tell him that he will be learning about the letter "Q" this week. Tell him that Q-tip starts with the letter "Q." Tell him another word that starts with the letter "Q," like queen, quail, and quilt. Sound out the letter "Q" for him, "*q, q, queen.*"

First, focus on tracing the letter "Q" with a Q-tip since that's the letter this week. Draw an uppercase Q for your child to trace a few times, and then draw a lowercase q for your child to trace a few times. When your child traces the letter it will most likely erase it, and that it perfectly fine. After he traces the "Q's" a few times, you can draw other letters or numbers for him to trace. (My son likes to tell me what letter or number to draw for him to trace.)

TUESDAY

LOW PREP *Make Quesadillas*

Materials

- ☐ Tortillas
- ☐ Cheese
- ☐ Griddle, Frying Pan, or Oven

Directions

Ask your toddler if he would like to make a yummy quesadilla. Tell him that the word "quesadilla" starts with the letter "Q." Sound it out for him, "*q, q, quesadilla.*" Let him repeat it back to you. You can place the tortilla in front of him, and let him spread cheese all over the tortilla. (We used cheddar cheese, but feel free to use any kind you would like.) Add other goodies like black beans, chicken, peppers, or onions to the quesadilla if your toddler Is interested. (I have a picky toddler, so we used only cheese.)

Once the quesadilla is ready, help your toddler fold the quesadilla in half. Now you can cook the quesadilla on a griddle, in a frying pan, or even in the oven. Heat it enough to make the cheese gooey and the tortilla toasty. Let your little one enjoy his tasty creation.

WEDNESDAY

Play in Quicksand

Materials

- ☐ Plastic Container
- ☐ Sand
- ☐ Water
- ☐ Small Toys

Directions

Get a plastic container, like a storage bin, and pour sand in it. Fill it half full with sand. Now ask your toddler if he wants to make quicksand to play in. Tell him that the word "quicksand" starts with the letter "Q." Ask him if he knows what sound the letter "Q" makes. Sound it out with him, "q, q, quicksand." Tell him that quicksand is made of sand and water. Let him feel the sand in the container. Now let him add a little bit of water to the sand. Talk to your toddler about how the sand changed when he added a little bit of water. Let him feel it. Now add enough water so that the water is covering the sand. Let him play in the quicksand. He can use his hands, shovels, and toys to explore the quicksand.

THURSDAY

LOW PREP ## Make a Q for Quail Picture

Materials

- ☐ Quail Activity Page (Appendix Al)
- ☐ Scissors
- ☐ Glue Stick
- ☐ Construction Paper
- ☐ Crayons
- ☐ Feather (Optional)

Directions

Let your toddler color each part of the *Quail* activity page. Cut out the pieces from the *Quail* activity page. Ask your toddler to pick out a piece of construction paper on which to glue the quail. Assemble the quail, unglued, on the construction paper so that your little one can see what the picture should look like when completed. Tell your toddler that quail starts with the letter "Q." Then tell him the sound, "q, q, quail." Ask him to repeat it back to you. Ask your toddler to help rub glue on each piece of the quail, and press the pieces onto the construction paper. Assist as needed. If you have a feather, cut a small piece off of the feather, and glue it to the top of the quail's head to complete the picture.

FRIDAY

Letter Q Mystery Bag

Materials

- ☐ 4 Objects that Start with the Letter Q (Ex. Quilt, Queen, Q-tip)
- ☐ 4 Objects that Start with a Different Letter (Ex. Glove, Hat, Cup)
- ☐ Duffle Bag

Directions

Put all eight objects in to the duffle bag. Tell your toddler that there are surprises in your bag. Explain that some surprises start with the letter "Q," and some surprises don't start with the letter "Q." Ask him to reach into your bag and pull out one surprise. Ask him what the object is that he pulled out. Say the name of the object together with your child, and sound out the first letter of the object's name together. Ask your toddler if the object starts with the letter "Q." If it does start with a "Q," put it in one pile, but if it doesn't start with the letter "Q," put it in a different pile.

For example, if your toddler pulls out a quilt. Ask him the name of the object. Next, you would say the word "quilt" together. Sound out the first letter of the word quilt to your toddler, "q, q, *quilt.*" Now ask your child if quilt starts with the letter "Q." After he answers, put the quilt in the "does start with Q" pile.

ALTERNATE ACTIVITY

LOW PREP Q-tip Shapes

Materials

- ☐ Half a Poster Board
- ☐ Marker
- ☐ Q-Tips
- ☐ Glue

Directions

Use your marker to draw shapes onto the poster board. You can draw a square, rectangle, triangle, diamond, etc. Refrain from drawing shapes with rounded edges because it will make it more difficult to fit the Q-tips. Make sure the edges of your shapes are long enough to fit a Q-tip.

Now ask your toddler if he would like to make shapes using Q-tips. Show him the poster board with shapes on it, and ask him which shape he would like to make first. Now tell him that he will glue a Q-tip down on the each edge of the shape to form the shape. (I drew a line of glue for my son on each shape, and then he would place the Q-tip on the glue.) Count how many Q-tips it takes to make each shape with your toddler.

The letter "R" sound can be difficult for a young child. There are two different ways place the tongue to create the "ruh" sound. Let your toddler experiment and find the most comfortable way for him.

MONDAY

LOW PREP *Make Straw Rockets*

Materials

- ☐ Rocket Activity Page (Appendix AJ)
- ☐ Scotch Tape
- ☐ Markers, Crayons, or Colored Pencils
- ☐ Scissors
- ☐ Straws

Directions

Tell your toddler that he will learn about the letter "R" this week, and today he gets to make straw rockets. Tell him that the word "rocket" starts with the letter "R." Sound out the letter "R" for him, "*r, r, rocket.*" Ask him to repeat it to you.

Now show your little one the *Rocket* activity page. Tell him that he can color the rockets with whatever color he chooses. Let him use markers, crayons or colored pencils to color the rockets. (My son only colored 2 lines because he was anxious to make the rockets fly.) When your little one is finished coloring, cut the rockets out. Now take two rockets and place them back to back. Place tape around the edges of the rocket. Do not tape the bottom of the rocket. You should be able to squeeze the sides of the rocket and the bottom of the rocket will open. After you tape the rocket, stick one end of the straw in the rocket. Tell your toddler to tilt his head back and place the other end of the straw in his mouth. Now tell your child to blow into the straw. The rocket should fly into the air. Flying the rocket will hopefully provide many moments of enjoyment for your child.

TUESDAY

LOW PREP *Make an R for Rooster Picture*

Materials

- ☐ Rooster Activity Page (Appendix AK)
- ☐ Scissors
- ☐ Glue Stick
- ☐ Construction Paper
- ☐ Crayons

Directions

Let your toddler color each part of the *Rooster* activity page. Cut out the pieces from the *Rooster* activity page. Ask your toddler to pick out a piece of construction paper on which to glue the rooster. Assemble the rooster, unglued, on the construction paper so your little one can see what the rooster should look like when completed. Tell your toddler that the word rooster starts with the letter "R." Tell him the sound, "*r, r, rooster.*" Ask him to repeat it back to you. Ask your toddler to help rub glue on each piece of the rooster, and press the pieces onto the construction paper. Assist your child as needed. After the rooster is complete, find a place to hang the picture so that your little one can be proud of his work.

WEDNESDAY

LOW PREP *Robot Size Order*

Materials

- ☐ Robot Activity Page (Appendix AL)
- ☐ Scissors

Directions

Cut out each robot from the *Robot* activity page. Now show your toddler all of the robots. Tell him that the word robot starts with the letter "R." Ask him if he knows what sound the letter "R" makes. Sound it out together, "*r, r, robot.*" Now ask your toddler to find the smallest robot. Place it in front of your child. Now ask him to find the next biggest robot. Place it next to the smallest one. Continue this until the robots are in order from smallest to biggest. Play this again putting the robots in order from biggest to smallest.

— **R** —

LOW PREP *Rainbow Matching*

THURSDAY

Materials

- ☐ Rainbow Activity Page (Appendix AM)
- ☐ Scissors

Directions

Cut out the rainbows from the *Rainbow* activity page. Ask your toddler if he would like to match rainbows. Ask him if he knows the first letter of the word rainbow. Next, ask him if he knows what sound the letter "R" makes. Sound it out together, "*r, r, rainbow.*"

Group all of the dotted rainbow halves together, and then group all of the numbered rainbow halves together. Ask your toddler to pick one of the dotted rainbow halves. Count the dots on the piece he picked together with your child. Now ask him to find the numbered rainbow half that matches the number he counted. Continue this until all of the rainbows are matched.

LEARNING ABC'S

FRIDAY

Letter R Mystery Bag

Materials

- ☐ 4 Objects that Start with the Letter R (Ex. Rocket, Ribbon, Radio)
- ☐ 4 Objects that Start with a Different Letter (Ex. Scarf, Fork, Leaf)
- ☐ Duffle Bag

Directions

Put all eight objects in to the duffle bag. Tell your toddler that there are surprises in your bag. Explain that some surprises start with the letter "R," and some surprises don't start with the letter "R." Ask him to reach into your bag and pull out one surprise. Ask him what the object is that he pulled out. Say the name of the object together with your child, and sound out the first letter of the object's name. Ask your toddler if the object starts with the letter "R." If it does start with the letter "R," put it in one pile, but if the word doesn't start with the letter "R" put it in a different pile.

For example, if your toddler pulls out a leaf. Ask him the name of the object. Now you would say the word "leaf" together. Sound out the first letter of the word leaf to your toddler, "*l, l, leaf.*" Next, ask him if leaf starts with the letter "R." After he answers, put the leaf in the "does not start with R" pile.

ALTERNATE ACTIVITY

Make Rain in a Jar

Materials

- ☐ Glass Jar
- ☐ Paper Plate or Bowl
- ☐ Ice
- ☐ Water
- ☐ Small Pot

Directions

Ask your little one if he would like to make rain. Tell him that rain starts with the letter "R." Ask him what sound the letter "R" makes. Make the sound together with your child, "*r, r, rain.*"

Now boil some water in a small pot. After the water has started boiling, add 2-3 inches of the boiling water to the glass jar. Instruct your little one not to touch the jar because it is hot. Instruct your toddler to place the paper plate on top of the jar—face up. Let the plate sit on the jar for a few minutes. Now let your toddler help you get 10 pieces of ice from the freezer and place them on the paper plate that is on top of the jar. Watch the jar and observe the rain forming on the bottom of the plate. When the drops get heavy they will fall off the plate like rain.

To make the letter "S" sound, place the tip of your tongue close to the back of your teeth without touching them. Blow air between your teeth to make a hissing sound, "sss."

MONDAY

LOW PREP *Make an S for Snake Picture*

Materials

- ☐ Snake Activity Page (Appendix AN)
- ☐ Scissors
- ☐ Glue Stick
- ☐ Construction Paper
- ☐ Crayons
- ☐ Paint (Optional)

Directions

Let your toddler color each part of the *Snake* activity page. Cut out the pieces from the *Snake* activity page. Ask your toddler to pick out a piece of construction paper on which to glue the snake. Assemble the snake, unglued, on the construction paper so that your little one can see what the snake should look like when completed. Tell your toddler the word snake starts with the letter "S." Then tell him the sound, "s, s, snake." Ask him to repeat it back to you. Ask your toddler to help rub glue on each piece of the snake, and press the pieces onto the construction paper. Assist your child as needed. Now have your toddler add some dots or squiggles to the snake using paint of his choice. After the snake is dry, find a place to hang the picture so your little one can be proud of his work.

TUESDAY

LOW PREP *Paint Squiggles*

Materials

- ☐ Sidewalk Chalk
- ☐ Paintbrush
- ☐ Cup of Water

Directions

This is a fun activity that helps toddlers develop their writing skills. Ask your toddler if he would like to go outside and paint squiggly lines. Tell him that the word squiggly starts with the letter "S." Ask him if he knows what sound the letter "S" makes. Sound it out together, "s, s, squiggly." Use the sidewalk chalk to draw dotted lines, zig zag lines, wavy lines, and straight lines. Next, show your toddler that he will dip the paint brush into the water and trace over the lines you made. Tell him that he will attempt to make the lines disappear. (My son really enjoyed this activity. He asked me to draw shapes and write his name so he could trace them too.)

LEARNING ABC'S

WEDNESDAY

LOW PREP *Star Counting*

Materials

- ☐ Star Stickers
- ☐ Index Cards
- ☐ Marker

Directions

Ask your toddler if he would like to count stars. Ask him if he knows the first letter in the word star. Ask him if he knows what sound the letter "S" makes. Sound it out together, "*s, s, star.*" Use your marker to write the numbers 1-10 on the index cards; each card should have one number on it. Lay the cards out in front of your toddler. Point to the number one card and ask him to tell you the number. Now ask him how many stars he should put on the card—it should be the same number. Hand him one sticker at a time to place on the card.

THURSDAY

LOW PREP *Make S'mores*

Materials

- ☐ Graham Crackers
- ☐ Big Marshmallows
- ☐ Chocolate Bars

Directions

(We made our s'mores in the oven, but you can roast your marshmallows over the fire if you have access to a fire.) Ask your toddler if he would like to make a s'more. (My son asked to make s'mores each day of S week.) Tell your toddler that s'more starts with the letter "S." Ask him if he knows what sound the letter "S" makes. Sound it out together, "*s, s, s'more.*"

Heat your oven to 350 degrees Fahrenheit. Take a cookie sheet from the cabinet. Let your little one lay the graham cracker squares on the cookie sheet. Next, ask him to place the chocolate bars on top of the graham crackers. (I used the Hershey's chocolate bars and broke them up so that each s'more had three pieces of chocolate.) Have your toddler place a marshmallow on top of the chocolate. Place the cookie sheet into the oven and let the s'mores cook between 5-10 minutes. The marshmallow should start to puff up, and the chocolate should start to melt. Be careful not to burn the chocolate. Take the s'more out of the oven. Place the remaining graham cracker on top of the marshmallow. Let the s'more cool for a couple of minutes before giving it to your toddler. Now you and your little one can enjoy your tasty s'mores!areful not to burn the chocolate. Now you and your little one can enjoy your tasty s'mores!

FRIDAY

Letter S Mystery Bag

Materials

- ☐ 4 Objects that Start with the Letter S (Ex. Strawberry, Stamp, Sock)
- ☐ 4 Objects that Start with a Different Letter (Ex. Paper, Train, Banana)
- ☐ Duffle Bag

Directions

Put all eight objects in to the duffle bag. Tell your toddler that there are surprises in your bag. Explain that some surprises start with the letter "S," and some surprises don't start with the letter "S." Ask him to reach into your bag and pull out one surprise. Ask him to name the he pulled out. Say the name of the object together, and sound out the first letter of the object's name together. Ask your toddler if the object starts with "S." If the object starts with the letter "S," put it in one pile. If the object doesn't start with the letter "S," put it in a different pile.

For example, if your toddler pulls out a sock. Ask him the name of the object. Next, you would say the word "sock" together. Sound out the first letter of the word sock to your toddler, "*s, s, sock*." Now ask him if the word sock starts with "S." After he answers, put the sock in the "does start with S" pile.

ALTERNATE ACTIVITY

Shape Puzzle

Materials

- ☐ Shape Puzzle Activity Page (Appendix AO)
- ☐ Scissors

Directions

Ask your toddler if he would like to do a puzzle. Tell him it is a puzzle with shapes. Tell him that the word "shape" starts with the letter "S." Ask him if he knows what sound the letter "S" makes. Sound the word out together with your child, "*s, s, shape*."

Cut out the shapes from the *Shape Puzzle* activity page. Tell your little one that he needs to match the shape to its shadow shape (the gray shapes). If your child needs help, show him an example.

The letter "T" sound is made similar as the letter "D" sound. It is a quick puff of air pushed through the mouth, "tuh."

MONDAY

Name Train

Materials

- ☐ Train Activity Page (Appendix AP)
- ☐ Scissors
- ☐ Crayons
- ☐ Marker

Directions

Tell your toddler that he will be learning about the letter "T" this week, and today he will get to make a name train. Tell him that "train" starts with the letter "T." Sound the word out for him, "*t, t, train.*" Ask him to repeat it back to you.

Using the *Train* activity page, ask your toddler to color the train with his crayons. When he is finished coloring, cut out the train cars—just cut out the number of cars you need for your toddler's name. (My son has six letters in his name, so I only used six train cars.) Now use your marker to write your toddler's name on the train cars. There should be one letter for each car. Put the name train in order for your toddler to read it. Show your child his name by saying and pointing to each letter. Say your child's name after you spell it. If you can spell your child's name to a little tune, that will help him learn it too. You can mix up the letters, and ask your toddler to spell his name. Your child may need a little guidance the first few times.

TUESDAY

LOW PREP ### Play Tennis

Materials

- ☐ 2 Fly Swatters
- ☐ Balloon

Directions

This activity can be played outside or inside if you have enough space. Ask your little one if he would like to play tennis. Tell him that the word "tennis" starts with the letter "T." Sound it out for him, "*t, t, tennis.*" Ask your toddler to repeat it back to you.

Blow up your balloon. Now show your toddler how he can hit the balloon to you with the fly swatter, and how you can hit it back to him.

WEDNESDAY

LOW PREP *Make a T for Tree Picture*

Materials

- ☐ Tree Activity Page (Appendix AQ)
- ☐ Scissors
- ☐ Glue Stick
- ☐ Construction Paper
- ☐ Crayons
- ☐ Green Paint (Optional)

Directions

Let your toddler color each part of the *Tree* activity page. Cut out the pieces from the *Tree* activity page. Ask your toddler to pick out a piece of construction paper on which to glue the tree. Assemble the tree, unglued, on the construction paper so your little one can see what the tree should look like when completed. Tell your toddler the word tree starts with the letter "T." Next, tell him the sound, "*t, t, tree.*" Ask him to repeat it back to you. Ask your toddler to help rub glue on each piece of the tree, and press the pieces onto the construction paper. Assist your child as needed. Ask your toddler to add some leaves to the tree using the green paint. He can dip his finger in the green paint and make dots across the top portion of the tree. After the tree is dry, find a place to hang the picture so that your little one can be proud of his work.

THURSDAY

Truck Patterns

Materials

- ☐ Truck Activity Page (Appendix AR)
- ☐ Scissors

Directions

Ask your toddler if he would like to make a "pattern" with trucks. Tell him that the word "truck" starts with the letter "T." Ask him if he knows what sound the letter "T" makes. Sound it out together with your child, "*t, t, truck.*" Cut out all of the trucks from the *Truck* activity page.

Group all of the blue trucks together and group all of the yellow trucks together. Show your toddler an example of a pattern by placing a blue truck, yellow truck, blue truck, and yellow truck in front of him   Describe the pattern to your child ("blue truck-yellow truck-blue truck...."), and ask him which truck comes next. Continue to say the pattern out loud to him, and ask him which truck comes next until all of the trucks are in the pattern. You can do this activity again with a different pattern; for example, yellow truck, blue truck, blue truck, yellow truck or all blue trucks.

LEARNING ABC'S

FRIDAY

Letter T Mystery Bag

Materials

- ☐ 4 Objects that Start with the Letter T (Ex. Train, Toothbrush, Tennis Ball)
- ☐ 4 Objects that Start with a Different Letter (Ex. Lotion, Crayon, Apple)
- ☐ Duffle Bag

Directions

Put all eight objects in to the duffle bag. Tell your toddler that there are surprises in your bag. Explain that some surprises start with the letter "T," and some surprises don't start with the letter "T." Ask him to reach into your bag and pull out one surprise. Ask him to tell you the name of the object he pulled out of the bag. Say the name of the object together with your child, and sound out the first letter of the object's name together. Ask your toddler if the object starts with the letter "T." If it does start with a "T," put it in one pile, but if it doesn't start with the letter "T," put it in a different pile.

For example, if your toddler pulls out a toothbrush. Ask him the name of the object. Next, you would say "toothbrush" together with your child. Sound out the first letter of toothbrush to your toddler, "*t, t, toothbrush.*" Now ask him if toothbrush starts with the letter "T." After he answers, put the toothbrush in the "does start with T" pile.

 # ALTERNATE ACTIVITY

Make a Turtle

Materials

- ☐ Green Construction Paper
- ☐ Paper Plate
- ☐ Green Paint
- ☐ Paintbrush
- ☐ Scissors
- ☐ Glue
- ☐ Marker

Directions

Ask your toddler if he would like to make a turtle. Ask him if he knows the first letter in the word "turtle." Next, ask him if he knows what sound the letter "T" makes. Sound it out together, "*t, t, turtle.*" Now ask your toddler to paint the entire paper plate green. You will want him to paint the bottom of the plate green—this will be the shell.

While the plate is drying cut out the head, feet, and tail from the green construction paper. Cut out a skinny triangle for the tail, and four small half ovals for the feet, and one big half oval for the head. Once the shell is dry, flip the plate over so the paint is on the bottom. Have your toddler assist you in gluing on the head, feet, and tail. Flip your turtle over, and allow your toddler to use the marker to draw eyes on the turtles head.

The letter "U" has two sounds. There is a long sound, "yuw" and a short sound, "uh." To make the short "U" sound the tongue needs to be relaxed and in the center of the mouth.

MONDAY

LOW PREP *Utensil Painting*

Materials

- ☐ Plastic Fork, Knife, and Spoon
- ☐ Paint
- ☐ Paper Plate
- ☐ Paper

Directions

Tell your toddler that he will learn about the letter "U" this week. Ask him if he would like to paint with utensils. Show him the utensils he will use in this painting activity—the plastic fork, knife and spoon. Tell him that the word "utensil" starts with the letter "U." The word utensil makes the long "U" sound. Sound it out for him, "*u, u, utensil.*" Ask him to repeat it back to you.

Let your toddler pick out a piece of paper, and then let him pick out three paint colors. (I recommend having a paint color for each utensil so the paints don't get mixed together.) Put a dab of each paint color on the paper plate. Let your toddler create a masterpiece using the utensils in the paint.

LOW PREP *Make a U for Umbrella Picture*

TUESDAY

Materials

- ☐ Umbrella Activity Page (Appendix AS)
- ☐ Scissors
- ☐ Glue Stick
- ☐ Construction Paper
- ☐ Crayons
- ☐ Blue Paint (Optional)

Directions

Let your toddler color each part of the *Umbrella* activity page. Cut out the pieces from the *Umbrella* activity page. Ask your toddler to pick out a piece of construction paper on which to glue the umbrella. Assemble the umbrella, unglued, on the construction paper so your little one can see how the umbrellas should look when completed. Tell your toddler that umbrella starts with the letter "U." The word umbrella makes the short "U" sound. Tell him the sound of the letter, "*u, u, umbrella.*" Ask him to repeat it back to you. Ask your toddler to help rub glue on each piece of the umbrella, and press the pieces onto the construction paper. Assist your child as needed. Ask your toddler to add rain drops to the picture using the blue paint. Your child can dip his finger in the blue paint and make dots all over the picture. After the umbrella is dry, find a place to hang the picture so your little one can be proud of his work.

LEARNING ABC'S

WEDNESDAY

LOW PREP *Throw a Balloon Up*

Materials

☐ Balloon

Directions

Ask your toddler if he would like to throw a balloon up into the air. Tell him that the word "up" starts with the letter "U." Ask him if he can tell you the sound that the letter "U" makes. Sound it out together with your child, "*u, u, up.*" Let your little one pick out a balloon. Blow up the balloon, and let him throw it up as many times as he would like. As he is throwing it up in the air, ask him to tell you the first letter in the word "up."

U

THURSDAY

U-Toss

Materials

☐ Paper Towel Tube
☐ Egg Carton
☐ Poster Board
☐ Scissors
☐ Marker

Directions

U-Toss is similar to the game of horse shoes. Take your paper towel tube and place it on top of your egg carton so that the tube is standing straight up. Trace around the tube with your marker. Remove the tube, and cut out the circle from the egg carton. Now, place the tube into the egg carton. This will be the base for U-Toss. Now you will make the "U's". Draw two, big block letter "U's" onto the poster board. The center of the "U" should be wide enough to fit around the paper towel tube. Cut the "U's" out.

Ask your toddler if he would like to play U-Toss. Show him how to take a "U" and ring it around the tube. As you play, talk with your toddler about different objects that start with the letter "U."

FRIDAY

Letter U Mystery Bag

Materials

- ☐ 4 Objects that Start with the Letter U (Ex. Umbrella, Utensil, Unicorn)
- ☐ 4 Objects that Start with a Different Letter (Ex. Paint, Ball, Stickers)
- ☐ Duffle Bag

Directions

Put all eight objects in to the duffle bag. Tell your toddler that there are surprises in your bag. Explain that some surprises start with the letter "U," and some surprises don't start with the letter "U." Ask him to reach into your bag and pull out one surprise. Ask him the name of the object he removed from the bag. Say the name of the object together, and sound out the first letter of the object's name together. Ask your toddler if the object starts with the letter "U." If it does start with the letter "U," put it in one pile, but if it doesn't start with the letter "U" put it in a different pile.

For example, if your toddler pulls out an umbrella. Ask him the name of the object. Next, you would say "umbrella" together with your child. Sound out the first letter of umbrella to your toddler, "*u, u, umbrella.*" Now ask him if umbrella starts with the letter "U." After he answers, put the umbrella in the "does start with U" pile.

ALTERNATE ACTIVITY

LOW PREP *Learn Positions, Like Under*

Materials

- ☐ 2 Cups
- ☐ Toy

Directions

For this activity select a small toy or action figure that your toddler enjoys playing with a lot. (My son loves cars, so we chose a Hot Wheels car for this activity.)

Tell your toddler that he is going to learn about positional words, like under. Tell him the word "under" starts with the letter "U." Ask him if he knows what sound the letter "U" makes. Sound it out together with your child, "*u, u, under.*" Now show your toddler that when you say the word "under," he needs to place the toy under the cup. With each positional word you say to your child, he will place the toy in that position in relation to the cup. You can use your cup to show him examples. Here is a list of positional words:

on, under, next to, in front of, behind, in between, around, above, beside

LEARNING ABC'S

To make the letter "V" sound, bring your bottom lip up to your top teeth so they are barely touching, "vuh."

MONDAY

Make Violins

Materials

- ☐ Nutter Butters
- ☐ Peanut Butter
- ☐ Pretzel Sticks
- ☐ Melted Chocolate
- ☐ Wax Paper
- ☐ Knife
- ☐ Small Bowl

Directions

Tell your toddler that he will be learning about the letter "V" this week, and today he will get to make little violins. Show him a short clip of someone playing a violin. Tell him the word "violin" starts with the letter "V." Sound it out for him, "*v, v, violin.*"

Melt the chocolate in a small bowl; you don't need much. (I just melted some chocolate chips in the microwave for a few seconds.) Lay out a big sheet of wax paper. Next, hand your toddler two pretzel sticks so he can dip the ends of the pretzel sticks into the melted chocolate. Ask your child to lay the pretzels on the wax paper right next to each other—these are the violin's handle. Your toddler can make as many violin handles as he would like. As the violin handles harden, ask your toddler to hand you the Nutter Butter cookies one at a time so you can spread a medium dab of peanut butter in the center of the cookie. Do this for every violin you are making. Once your melted chocolate has hardened, ask your toddler to place the violin handle onto the violin (Nutter Butter). Place the end of the pretzel without chocolate onto the dab of peanut butter. Now you can place a pretzel stick with the violin as your bow. Enjoy your tasty violins!

Make a Volcano

Materials

- ☐ Baking Soda
- ☐ Vinegar
- ☐ Red Food Coloring
- ☐ Cookie Sheet with Edges
- ☐ Paper Lunch Bag
- ☐ Scissors
- ☐ Tape
- ☐ Plastic Cup
- ☐ Disposable Bowl

TUESDAY

Directions

Ask your toddler if he would like to make a volcano. Tell him the word "volcano" starts with the letter "V." Ask him if he knows what sound the letter "V" makes. Sound it out together, "*v, v, volcano.*"

Take your plastic cup and let your toddler add a rolled up piece of tape to the bottom of it. Now let your little one stick the cup inside the bowl. Place the bowl and cup into the paper lunch bag horizontally. Tape the opening of the bag underneath the bowl. It should look like the shape of a volcano when you're finished. Cut a circle on top of the bag, above the cup, so the volcano has an opening. Place your volcano on the cookie sheet to prevent a mess. Now pour baking soda into the cup—any amount. Ask your toddler to add red food coloring to the cup. Next, ask your toddler to pour vinegar into the cup, and watch the volcano erupt. (We had a better eruption by pouring the vinegar in the cup first and then adding baking soda but feel free to try different ways.)

WEDNESDAY

LOW PREP *Make a V for Vulture Picture*

Materials

- ☐ Vulture Activity Page (Appendix AT)
- ☐ Scissors
- ☐ Glue Stick
- ☐ Construction Paper
- ☐ Crayons

Directions

Let your toddler color each part of the *Vulture* activity page. Cut out the pieces from the *Vulture* activity page. Ask your toddler to pick out a piece of construction paper on which to glue the vulture. Assemble the vulture, unglued, on the construction paper so that your little one can see what the vulture should look like when the activity is completed. Tell your toddler that the word "vulture" starts with the letter "V." Tell them the sound, "*v, v, vulture.*" Ask him to repeat it back to you. Ask your toddler to help rub glue on each piece of the vulture, and press the pieces onto the construction paper. Assist your child as needed. After the vulture is complete, find a place to hang the picture so your little one can be proud of his work.

Vegetable Taste Test

Materials

- ☐ Assortment of Vegetables
- ☐ Plate
- ☐ Knife

Directions

Ask your toddler if he would like to taste some yummy vegetables. Tell him the word "vegetable" starts with the letter "V." Ask him if he knows what sound the letter "V" makes. Sound it out with him, "*v, v, vegetables.*" Pick a variety of vegetables that you think your toddler would like to eat. (I chose vegetables that were in season; therefore, they were on sale. We tried squash, zucchini, yellow bell pepper, cucumber, and carrots.) Chop up each vegetable, and give him a slice as well as, yourself a slice. Maybe you will find a new vegetable that your toddler likes to eat! Periodically, while eating the various vegetables with your child, ask him to tell you the first letter in the word vegetable. Continue to pronounce the letter and word, "*v, v, vegetable.*"

THURSDAY

FRIDAY

Letter V Mystery Bag

Materials

- ☐ 4 Objects that Start with the Letter V (Ex. Vase, Violin, Vegetable)
- ☐ 4 Objects that Start with a Different Letter (Ex. Bowl, Block, Action Figure)
- ☐ Duffle Bag

Directions

Put all eight objects in to the duffle bag. Tell your toddler that there are surprises in your bag. Explain that some surprises start with the letter "V," and some surprises don't start with the letter "V." Ask him to reach into your bag and pull out one surprise. Ask him the name of the object. Say the name of the object together with your child, and sound out the first letter of the object's name together. Ask your toddler if the object starts with the letter "V." If it does start with a "V," put it in one pile, but if it doesn't start with the letter "V" put it in a different pile.

For example, if your toddler pulls out a bowl. Ask him the name of the object. Next, say the word "bowl" together with your child. Sound out the first letter of bowl to your toddler, "*b, b, bowl.*" Ask him if the word bowl starts with the letter "V." After he answers, put the bowl in the "does not start with V" pile.

 # ALTERNATE ACTIVITY

LOW PREP *Vacuum the Floor*

Materials

- ☐ Vacuum

Directions

Ask your toddler if he would like to help you vacuum the floor. Tell your toddler the word "vacuum" starts with the letter "V." Tell him the sound it makes, "*v, v, vacuum.*" Ask him to repeat it back to you. Take the vacuum out, plug it in, and show your little one that you move the vacuum back and forth. Let him try.

The letter "W" makes a "wuh" sound. To make the sound, your lips come together to make a tight round shape.

MONDAY

Make a Windsock

Materials

- ☐ Half a Piece of Poster Board
- ☐ Stapler
- ☐ Paint, Crayons, or Colored Pencils
- ☐ Streamers or Ribbon
- ☐ Scissors
- ☐ Single Hole Punch
- ☐ String or Yarn

Directions

Tell your toddler that he will be learning about the letter "W" this week, and today he will make a windsock. Tell him a windsock moves when the wind blows. Tell him that the word "windsock" starts with the letter "W." Sound it out for him, "w, w, windsock." Ask him to repeat it back to you.

Let your toddler decorate the poster board using paint, crayons, or colored pencils. He can even use stickers. When he is finished decorating, bring both ends of the poster board together to make a cylinder, and use the stapler to staple the ends together. The pretty decorations should be on the outside of the cylinder. Now cut streamers or ribbon, eight inches long. (Our windsock held eight pieces of ribbon, so you might need eight, eight inch pieces of streamers or ribbon for your windsock.) Once you have the ribbon cut, place an end of the ribbon inside the bottom of the cylinder and let your toddler staple it in place. Now turn the cylinder a little bit, and staple the next piece of ribbon to the inside of the cylinder. Continue until there are ribbon pieces all around the cylinder. Now let your toddler punch a hole into the top of the cylinder, and another hole directly across from the first hole. Tie a string through the holes so you have something to hang up the windsock. Let your toddler choose a place outside to hang his windsock. You might want to encourage your child to put it close to a window so he can observe it when he is inside.

TUESDAY

LOW PREP ### Watermelon Counting

Materials

- ☐ Watermelon Activity Pages (Appendix AU)
- ☐ Black Beans

Directions

Ask your toddler if he would like to count watermelon seeds. Tell him the word "watermelon" starts with the letter "W." Sound it out for him, "w, w, watermelon." Cut out the watermelon on the *Watermelon* activity pages, and lay them in front of your toddler. Count the watermelons together. Starting at the number one, ask your toddler what number is on the watermelon. Next, ask how many watermelon seeds he needs to put on the watermelon (it should be the number he said). Now ask your child to count with you the correct number of black beans to place on the watermelon. Do this for each watermelon.

LEARNING ABC'S

WEDNESDAY

LOW PREP *Make a W for Wagon Picture*

Materials

- ☐ Wagon Activity Page (Appendix AV)
- ☐ Scissors
- ☐ Glue Stick
- ☐ Construction Paper
- ☐ Crayons

Directions

Let your toddler color each part of the *Wagon* activity page. Cut out the pieces from the *Wagon* activity page. Ask your toddler to pick out a piece of construction paper on which to glue the wagon. Assemble the wagon, unglued, on the construction paper so your little one can see what the wagon should look like when completed. Tell your toddler that wagon starts with the letter "W." Tell him the sound, "*w, w, wagon.*" Ask him to repeat it back to you. Ask your toddler to help rub glue on each piece of the wagon, and press the pieces onto the construction paper. Assist your child as needed.

Make a Whale Snack

THURSDAY

Materials

- ☐ 6 oz Vanilla Yogurt
- ☐ Blue Food Coloring
- ☐ Banana
- ☐ Vanilla Wafers
- ☐ Chocolate Chips
- ☐ Knife
- ☐ Plate

Directions

Ask your toddler if he would like to help you make a whale snack. Tell him that the word "whale" starts with the letter "W." Ask him if he knows what sound the letter "W" makes. Sound it out together, "*w, w, whale.*"

Ask your little one to put a few drops of blue food coloring in the yogurt. Stir the mixture until it is all blue. Now place the yogurt in the center of a plate. Take a banana and cut it in half. Place the banana on the yogurt. Ask your toddler to stick a chocolate chip just behind the cut end, on both sides. These are the whale's eyes. Now cut a vanilla wafer in half, and then cut one of those halves in half. Take the quartered vanilla wafers and ask your toddler to stick them in the sides of the banana, about in the middle. These are the whale's flippers. Next, take the halved vanilla wafer and ask your toddler to stick the rounded end into the very end of the banana. This is the whale's tail. Now your toddler can enjoy a whale of a treat!!

FRIDAY

Letter W Mystery Bag

Materials

- ☐ 4 Objects that Start with the Letter W (Ex. Watermelon, Water Bottle, Washcloth)
- ☐ 4 Objects that Start with a Different Letter (Ex. Key, Carrot, Flower)
- ☐ Duffle Bag

Directions

Put all eight objects in to the duffle bag. Tell your toddler that there are surprises in your bag. Explain that some surprises start with the letter "W," and some surprises don't start with the letter "W." Ask him to reach into your bag and pull out one surprise. Ask him the name of the object he removed from the bag. Say the name of the object together, and sound out the first letter of the object's name together. Ask your toddler if the object starts with the letter "W." If it does start with the letter "W," put it in one pile, but if it doesn't start with the letter "W," put it in a different pile.

For example, if your toddler pulls out a key. Ask him the name of the object. Next, you would say the word "key" together. Sound out the first letter of key to your toddler, "k, k, key." Now ask him if the word "key" starts with the letter "W." After he answers, put the key in the "does not start with W" pile.

ALTERNATE ACTIVITY

Make a Walrus Puppet

Materials

- ☐ Brown Paper Lunch Bag
- ☐ Brown Construction Paper
- ☐ White Construction Paper
- ☐ Scissors
- ☐ Glue
- ☐ Brown Yarn or Pipe Cleaners
- ☐ Black Marker
- ☐ Handles of a Plastic Utens or White Pipe Cleaner

Directions

Ask your toddler if he would like to make a walrus puppet. Tell him that the word "walrus" starts with the letter "W." Ask him if he knows what sound the letter "W" makes. Sound it out with him, "w, w, walrus."

Place the brown paper bag in front of him with the bottom flap face up. You will need to cut out a peanut shaped cheek from the brown construction paper. It needs to be as wide as the bag, and as tall as half of the flap. Now let your toddler glue it onto the flap of the brown paper bag. Cut out two white circles from the white construction paper—about an inch in diameter. Let your toddler glue the eyes above the cheeks. Now ask your toddler to take the black marker and put black dots in the white circles for the walrus's eyes. Next, help him draw a nose and mouth in the center of the cheeks on the walrus. Cut the brown string or the pipe cleaners into eight, two inch pieces. These will be the walrus's whiskers. Help your toddler glue them onto the cheeks. Now you can break the ends of two plastic forks, so you are left with the handles. Lift up the flap and glue the handles to the underside of the flap. These are the walrus's tusks. You can use white pipe cleaners if you do not have plastic utensils. The pipe cleaners and fork handles might need to be glued down with a hot glue gun. When the walrus is complete, let your little one play with his new walrus.

LEARNING ABC'S

The letter "X" has a unique sound, "ks."

MONDAY

LOW PREP X-Ray Hands

Materials

- [ ] Black Construction Paper
- [ ] White Crayon
- [ ] Q-Tips
- [ ] Glue

Directions

Explain to your little one that he will be learning about the letter "X" this week, and today he will make x-rays. Tell him that the word "x-ray" starts with the letter "X."

Tell your toddler that doctors use x-rays to take pictures of bones, so he is going to make a picture of his pretend bones. Have your child lay his hand on the black paper, enabling you to trace it. Trace his hand and half way up his forearm with the white crayon. Now tell your toddler he has bones in his fingers and arms. Let him feel the bones if he would like to do so. Put a line of glue in each traced finger and let your toddler place a Q-tip on the glue. Place two lines of glue parallel down the forearm and let your toddler place Q-tips on the glue.

TUESDAY

LOW PREP Make a Xylophone Snack

Materials

- [ ] Graham Crackers
- [ ] M&M's
- [ ] Pretzel Sticks
- [ ] Mini Marshmallows
- [ ] Icing
- [ ] Ziploc Sandwich Bag
- [ ] Scissors

Directions

Ask your toddler if he would like to make a xylophone snack. Tell him the word "xylophone" starts with the letter "X." Sound it out for him, "x, x, xylophone." Ask him to repeat it back to you.

Take a scoop or two of icing and put it into your Ziploc sandwich bag. Squeeze it down into one corner, and cut off the very tip of the bag. You now have a cake decorating bag. Place the rectangle graham cracker in front of your toddler. Let your toddler use the icing to draw six lines across the width of the graham cracker. The first line needs to be long enough to stick two M&M's to it; the second, third, and fourth lines need to be long enough to stick three M&M's to it; and the fifth and sixth lines need to be long enough to stick four M&M's to it. Let your toddler pick one color of M&M's for each line of icing. Place the M&M's on each line of icing. When your child has placed all of his M&M's on the xylophone, you can make the mallets by taking two pretzel sticks and sticking a mini marshmallow on the end of each pretzel. Let your child pretend to play his xylophone, and then he can enjoy a snack.

WEDNESDAY

LOW PREP *X Marks the Spot Patterns*

Materials

- ☐ X Marks the Spot Activity Page (Appendix AW)
- ☐ Scissors

Directions

Ask your toddler if he would like to make "X" patterns. Ask him if he knows what sound the letter "X" makes. Cut out the *X Marks the Spot* activity page patterns and the answer options. Show your toddler one pattern and say the pattern to him. Now, ask him to pick the correct "X" that would finish the pattern to place in the box. Do this until each pattern is complete.

LOW PREP *Make an X for Xylophone Picture*

Materials

- ☐ Xylophone Activity Page (Appendix AX)
- ☐ Scissors
- ☐ Glue Stick
- ☐ Construction Paper
- ☐ Crayons
- ☐ Black Paint (Optional)

THURSDAY

Directions

Let your toddler color each part of the *Xylophone* activity page. Cut out the pieces from the *Xylophone* activity page. Ask your toddler to pick out a piece of construction paper on which to glue the xylophone. Assemble the xylophone, unglued, on the construction paper so that your little one can see what the xylophone looks like when completed. Tell your toddler that the word "xylophone" starts with the letter "X." Next, tell him the sound, "*x, x, xylophone.*" Ask him to repeat it back to you. Ask your toddler to help rub glue on each piece of the xylophone, and press the pieces onto the construction paper. Assist your child as needed. Now add black paint dots to each end of the xylophone keys to look like the bolts that hold the keys in place. After the xylophone is complete, find a place to hang the picture so your little one can be proud of his work.

LEARNING ABC'S

FRIDAY

Letter X Mystery Bag

Materials

- ☐ 4 Objects that Start with the Letter X (Ex. X-ray Fish, Xylophone, Xolo)
- ☐ 4 Objects that Start with a Different Letter (Ex. Hat, Lego, Tomato)
- ☐ Duffle Bag

Directions

Put all eight objects in to the duffle bag. Tell your toddler that there are surprises in your bag. Explain that some surprises start with the letter "X," and some surprises don't start with the letter "X." Ask him to reach into your bag and pull out one surprise. Ask them the name of the object he removed from the bag. Say the name of the object together, and sound out the first letter of the object's name together. Ask your toddler if the object starts with the letter "X." If it does start with the letter "X," put it in one pile, but if it doesn't start with the letter "X," put it in a different pile.

For example, if your toddler pulls out an X-ray fish, ask him the name of the object. Next, you would say the word "x-ray fish" together with your child. Sound out the first letter of the word "x-ray fish" to your toddler, "x, x, x-ray fish." Now ask him if x-ray fish starts with the letter "X." After he answers, put the x-ray fish in the "does start with X" pile.

 # ALTERNATE ACTIVITY

Paper Towel X-ray

Materials

- ☐ Paper Towel
- ☐ Cup
- ☐ Water
- ☐ Black Food Coloring
- ☐ Elmer's Glue
- ☐ Marker
- ☐ Paintbrush or Dropper

Directions

Ask your toddler if he wants to make an x-ray. Ask him if he knows what sound the letter "X" makes. Sound it out together with your child, "x, x, x-ray." Fill a cup halfway full of water, and add black food coloring—the darker, the better. Fold the paper towel in half, and unfold it. Now, trace your toddler's hand onto a paper towel with a marker onto one half of the paper towel. Let him use the glue bottle to trace over your tracing. Encourage your child to add bones or fun designs onto the paper towel with the glue if he would like to be creative. When your child is finished with the glue, take the other half of the paper towel and fold it over the glue lines. Let your little one press it firmly. Now he can add the x-ray ink. Let him paint or drip the x-ray ink all over the paper towel. The bones will start to show through the ink.

 LEARNING ABC'S

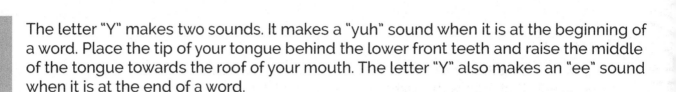
The letter "Y" makes two sounds. It makes a "yuh" sound when it is at the beginning of a word. Place the tip of your tongue behind the lower front teeth and raise the middle of the tongue towards the roof of your mouth. The letter "Y" also makes an "ee" sound when it is at the end of a word.

MONDAY

Yarn Maze

Materials

☐ Yarn   ☐ Tape   ☐ Scissors

Directions

Set the maze up beforehand. Pick a hallway or part of a room to set up your maze. (It's more of an obstacle course, but we are going to call it a maze.) We don't really have a hallway in our home, so I set up our kitchen chairs to be a hallway. Tie one end of the yarn to the chair leg or tape it to the wall, and weave it in and out of the chair legs at different heights to make a maze. Your toddler should have to crawl, step over, or slither through the yarn maze.

Ask your toddler if he would like to go through a yarn maze. Tell him that he will be learning about the letter "Y" this week, and that the word "yarn" starts with the letter "Y." Tell him the sound that the letter "Y" makes, "y, y, yarn." (I put a toy at the end of the yarn maze and told my son to climb through the yarn maze to get the toy, and bring it back to me.)

TUESDAY

LOW PREP ### Make a Y for Yak Picture

Materials

☐ Yak Activity Page (Appendix AY)   ☐ Construction Paper
☐ Scissors   ☐ Crayons
☐ Glue Stick

Directions

Let your toddler color each part of the *Yak* activity page. Cut out the pieces from the *Yak* activity page. Ask your toddler to pick out a piece of construction paper on which to glue the yak. Assemble the yak, unglued, on the construction paper so that your little one can see what the yak should look like when completed. Tell your toddler that the word "yak" starts with the letter "Y." Tell him the sound, "y, y, yak." Ask him to repeat it back to you. Ask your toddler to help rub glue on each piece of the yak, and press the pieces onto the construction paper. Assist your child as needed. After the yak is complete, find a place to hang the picture so that your little one can be proud of their work.

WEDNESDAY

Make a Yo-Yo

Materials

- ☐ 2 Paper Plates
- ☐ Crayons, Paint, Stickers, or Colored Pencils
- ☐ Glue
- ☐ Toilet Paper Tube
- ☐ Yarn
- ☐ Scissors
- ☐ Tape

Directions

Ask your little one if he would like to make a yo-yo. Tell him that the word "yo-yo" starts with the letter "Y." Ask him if he knows what sound the letter "Y" makes. Sound it out with him, "*y, y, yo-yo.*"

Let your toddler decorate the paper plates using stickers, crayons, paint, or anything he would like to use. You will need to wait for the plates to dry if he uses paint. After the plates are decorated, turn them face down. Cut your toilet paper tube in half. It should still be a tube, but just a smaller tube. Place a ring of glue around one end of the toilet paper tube, and then place it on the center of one of the face down plates. Now place a ring of glue on the other end of the toilet paper tube, and let your toddler place the other plate face up on top of the tube. Let it dry for five minutes. Now cut a piece of yarn—the height of your toddler. Tape one end of the yarn to the toilet paper tube and wrap it around the tube. Tie a little finger loop in the other end of the yarn, so your toddler can play with the yo-yo.

LOW PREP ## Make Yogurt Drops

THURSDAY

Materials

- ☐ Cookie Sheet
- ☐ Wax Paper
- ☐ Yogurt
- ☐ Sprinkles (Optional)
- ☐ Ziploc Sandwich Bag
- ☐ Scissors

Directions

Ask your toddler if he would like to make yogurt drops as a yummy treat. Tell your toddler that the word "yogurt" starts with the letter "Y." Ask him if he knows what sound the letter "Y" makes. Sound it out together with your child, "*y, y, yogurt.*" Place a piece of wax paper on your cookie sheet. Scoop the yogurt into your Ziploc bag, and squeeze it down into one corner. Cut the very tip of the corner off. Show your toddler how you can squeeze the bag and make little drops of yogurt onto the cookie sheet. Let your little one try a few drops. (I had to hold the bag and move it while my son squeezed.) When you finish making the yogurt drops, ask your toddler to add some sprinkles on top of the drops. Now set the cookie sheet in the freezer. After the yogurt drops have had time to freeze, you and your toddler can enjoy a refreshing treat.

FRIDAY

Letter Y Mystery Bag

Materials

- ☐ 4 Objects that Start with the Letter Y (Ex. Yo-yo, Yogurt, Yarn)
- ☐ 4 Objects that Start with a Different Letter (Ex. Leaf, Tape, Rock)
- ☐ Duffle Bag

Directions

Put all eight objects in to the duffle bag. Tell your toddler that there are surprises in your bag. Explain that some surprises start with the letter "Y," and some surprises don't start with the letter "Y." Ask him to reach into your bag and pull out one surprise. Ask him to tell you the name of the object you removed from the bag. Say the name of the object together with your child, and sound out the first letter of the object's name together. Ask your toddler if the object starts with the letter "Y." If it does start with the letter "Y," put it in one pile, but if it doesn't start with the letter "Y," put it in a different pile.

For example, if your toddler pulls out a rock. Ask him the name of the object. Next, say the word "rock" together with your child. Sound out the first letter of rock to your toddler, "*r, r, rock*." Now ask him if the word rock starts with the letter "Y." After he answers, put the rock in the "does not start with Y" pile.

ALTERNATE ACTIVITY

LOW PREP Wrap Yarn Around Y

Materials

- ☐ Cardboard
- ☐ Scissors
- ☐ Tape
- ☐ Yarn

Directions

Cut out a letter "Y" from cardboard. (I just used cardboard from a box we had.) Your "Y" should be the size of a piece of notebook paper. Tape one end of the yarn to the backside of the "Y," and wrap the yarn around the "Y" a couple of times. Ask your toddler if he would like to wrap the "Y" in yarn. Ask him if he knows the first letter in the word "yarn." Ask him if he knows what sound the letter "Y" makes. Sound it out with him, "*y, y, yarn*." Tell him that he will take the yarn and wrap it around the "Y." He can wrap it in any direction he wants. Let him hold the big spool of yarn as he wraps the "Y," and you can cut it when he has completed the wrapping. If your child is too young to handle this task safely simply cut a big piece of yarn off the spool for him to use to wrap the "Y." Tie the end of the yarn when he finishes his wrapping of the letter, or leave it loose so he can unwrap the "Y" and do the activity again.

MONDAY

To create the letter "Z" sound, place the front of the tongue close to the tooth ridge—close to the upper backside of the top front teeth, "zuh."

LOW PREP *Make a Z for Zebra Picture*

Materials

- ☐ Zebra Activity Page (Appendix AZ)
- ☐ Scissors
- ☐ Glue stick
- ☐ Construction Paper
- ☐ Crayons

Directions

Let your toddler color each part of the *Zebra* activity page. Cut out the pieces from the *Zebra* activity page. Ask your toddler to pick out a piece of construction paper on which to glue the zebra. Assemble the zebra, unglued, on the construction paper so your little one can see what the zebra will look like when the project is complete. Tell your toddler that "zebra" starts with the letter "Z." Next, tell him the sound, "*z, z, zebra.*" Ask him to repeat it back to you. Ask your toddler to help rub glue on each piece of the zebra, and press the pieces onto the construction paper. Assist your child as needed. After the zebra is complete, find a place to hang the picture so that your little one can be proud of his work.

LOW PREP *Zip Jackets*

TUESDAY

Materials

- ☐ Jackets

Directions

Ask your toddler if he would like to zip jackets. Tell him the word "zip" starts with the letter "Z." Sound it out for him, "*z, z, zip.*" Ask him to repeat it back to you. You can place a variety of jackets in front of your toddler and let him zip them up. My son liked to put the jackets on to zip them. (I usually had to get the zipper started, and then he would zip it all the way up and unzip it.) Let your toddler practice this skill as many times as he finds enjoyable.

   LEARNING ABC'S

WEDNESDAY

Zigzag Race

Materials

- ☐ Sidewalk Chalk
- ☐ Toy Cars (Optional)

Directions

Ask your toddler if he would like to have a zigzag race with you. Tell him that the word "zigzag" starts with the letter "Z." Ask him if he knows what sound the letter "Z" makes. Sound it out with him, "z, z, zigzag." Go outside and draw two racing lanes using the sidewalk chalk. However, instead of drawing straight racing lanes these are going to be zigzag racing lanes. Draw a start line at the beginning and a finish line at the end. Show your toddler how to run in a zigzag manner. Let him practice, and then you can have a race against each other. In addition, you can use toy cars to have a zigzag race. If you cannot use sidewalk chalk, tape zigzag lanes on your floor; (this is what we do if it is raining).

Z

THURSDAY

LOW PREP ### Make a Zebra Mask

Materials

- ☐ Paper Plate
- ☐ Black Crayon
- ☐ Pink Crayon
- ☐ Black Construction Paper
- ☐ White Construction Paper
- ☐ Scissors
- ☐ Tape
- ☐ Glue
- ☐ Popsicle Stick

Directions

Ask your toddler if he would like to make a zebra mask. Ask him if he knows the first letter in the word "zebra.". Ask him if he knows what sound the letter "Z" makes. Sound it out together with your child, "z, z, zebra."

First, cut out two eye holes from the center of the paper plate. Draw zebra stripes on either side of the eye holes. (I drew three triangles on each side for the stripes.) Let your toddler color the stripes black. (My son decided to draw his own stripes, and that was perfectly fine.) Cut out a circle from the black construction paper for the snout. Let your toddler glue the snout under the eyes. Cut out a strip of black construction paper, about two inches wide by three inches long. Next, cut slits along the three inch side, ¾ of the way down. This will be the mane. Now cut out two triangles from the white construction paper for the ears. Draw pink triangles in the ears, and let your toddler use the pink crayon to color them in. Now turn the plate over, and let your toddler glue the ears and mane to the top of the plate. Place the popsicle stick at the bottom of the backside of the plate and tape it in place. Now you have a cute little zebra!

FRIDAY

Letter Z Mystery Bag

Materials

- ☐ 4 Objects that Start with the Letter Z (Ex. Zipper, Zebra, Ziploc Bag)
- ☐ 4 Objects that Start with a Different Letter (Ex. Headphones, Lotion, Goggles)
- ☐ Duffle Bag

Directions

Put all eight objects in to the duffle bag. Tell your toddler that there are surprises in your bag. Explain that some surprises start with the letter "Z," and some surprises don't start with the letter "Z." Ask him to reach into your bag and pull out one surprise. Ask him the name of the object he removed from the bag. Say the name of the object together with your child, and sound out the first letter of the object's name together. Ask your toddler if the object starts with the letter "Z." If it does start with the letter "Z," put it in one pile, but if it doesn't start with the letter "Z," put it in a different pile.

For example, if your toddler pulls out a zipper, ask him the name of the object. Next, you would say "zipper" together with your child. Sound out the first letter of zipper to your toddler, "z, z, zipper." Now ask him if zipper starts with the letter "Z." After he answers, put the zipper in the "does start with Z" pile.

ALTERNATE ACTIVITY

Zebra Tracks

Materials

- ☐ Zebra Track Activity Page (Appendix BA)
- ☐ Sidewalk Chalk

Directions

Ask your little one if he would like to go outside and follow zebra tracks. Ask him if he knows the first letter in the word "zebra." Next, ask your child if he knows what sound the letter "Z" makes. Sound it out together with your child, "z, z, zebra." Now make zebra tracks. If you need guidance in making your own zebra tracks, use the *Zebra Track* activity page as a reference. Use sidewalk chalk to draw zebra tracks on the sidewalk. Draw the tracks in different colors, in a zig zag, in a straight line, or number them. Now let your toddler follow the zebra tracks. He can jump on them, count them, walk on them, or run on them. This can also be a fun "movement activity" for you and your child.

Appendix

To print a colored appendix, please visit:
www.BestMomIdeas.com/sendmyabcprintouts
Password: bestmomideas31a8

(Hint: I found it easier to print the appendix pages than to copy or tear them from the bound book ☺)

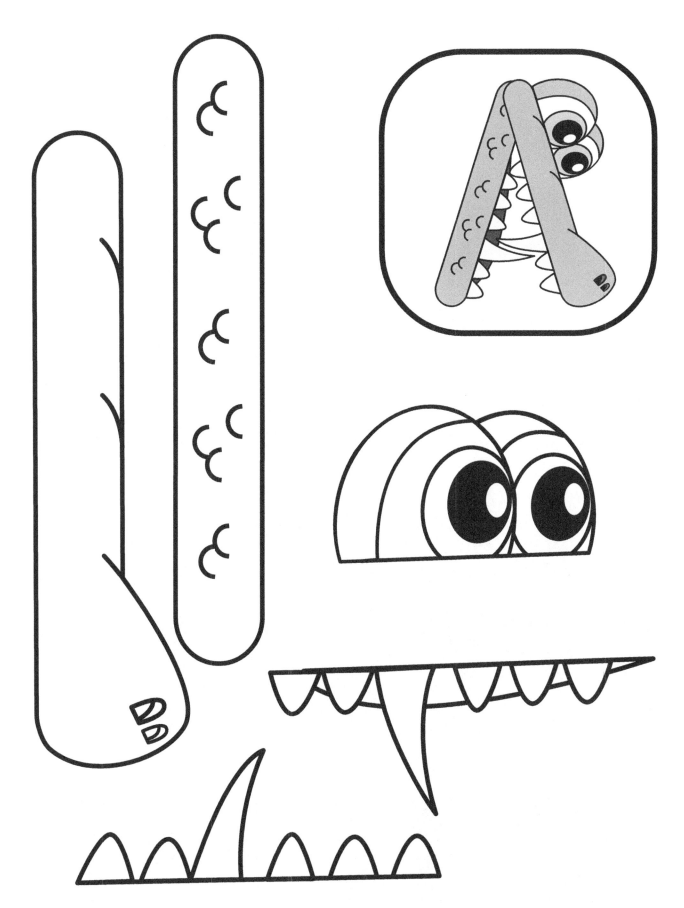

cut along line

cut along line

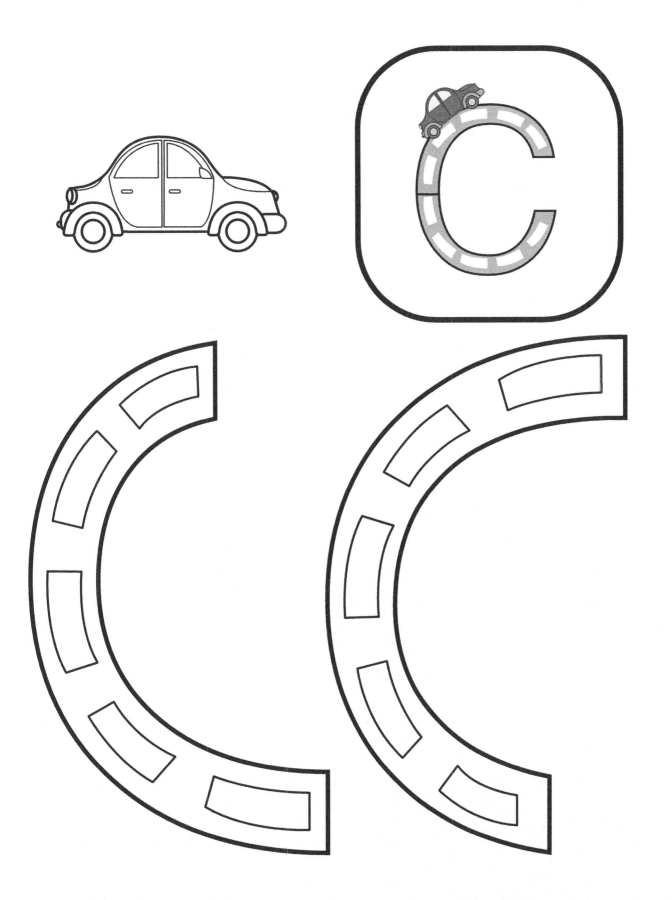

cut along line

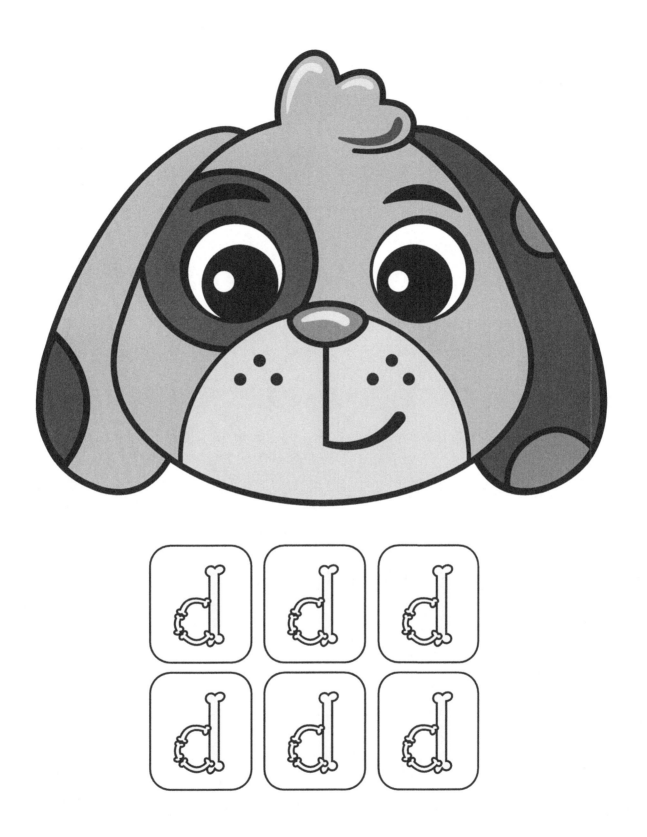

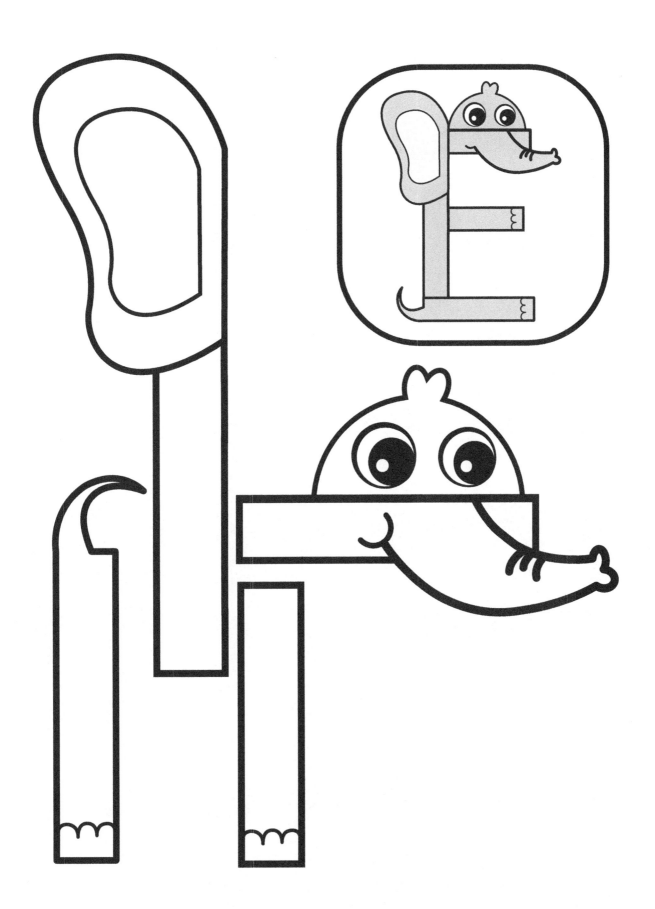

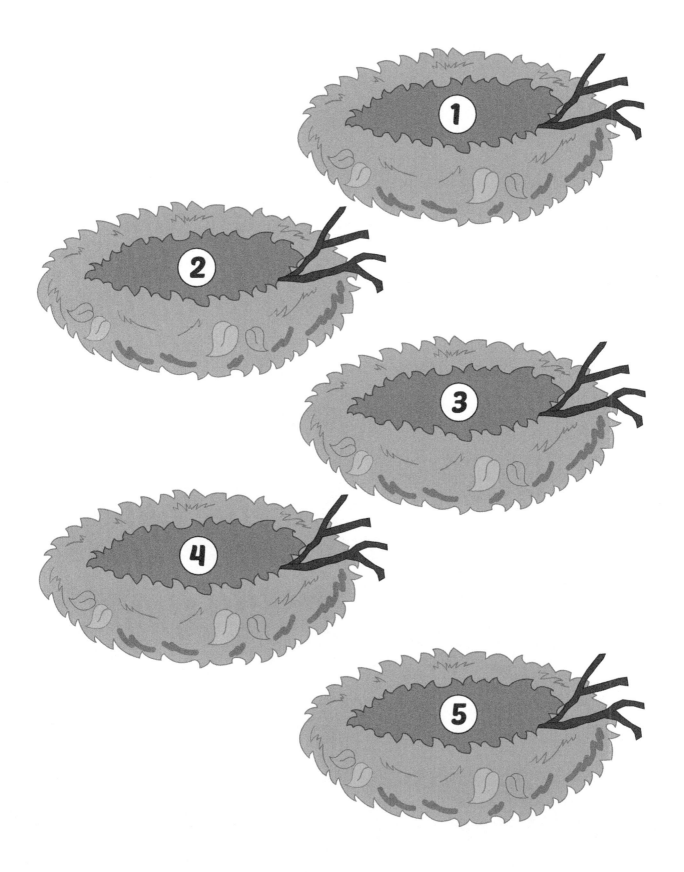

cut along line

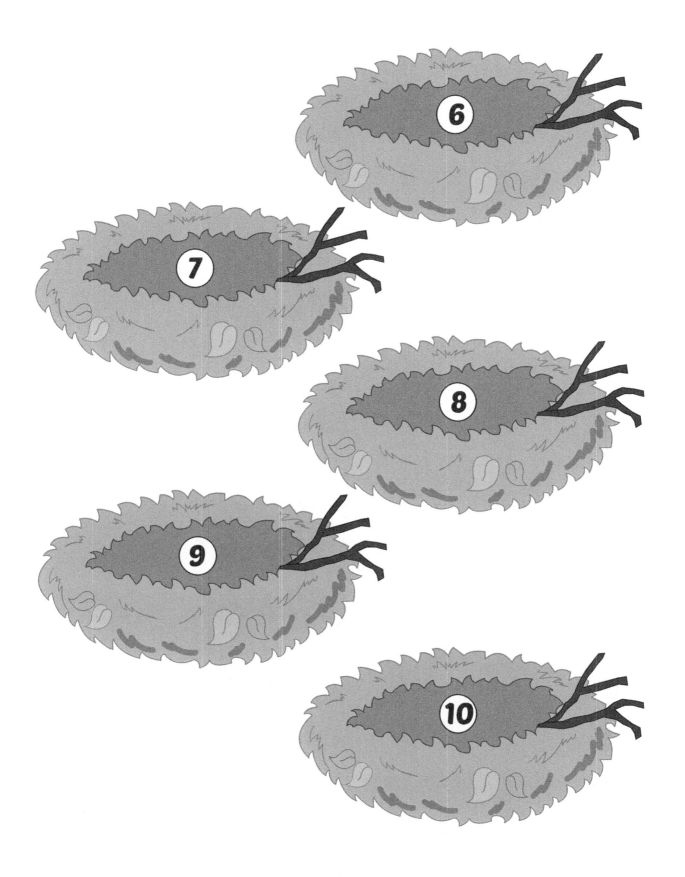

Five little speckled frogs, sitting on a mossy log.
Eating the most delicious bugs,
Yum! Yum!
One jumped into the pool,
where it was nice and cool.
Now there are four speckled frogs.

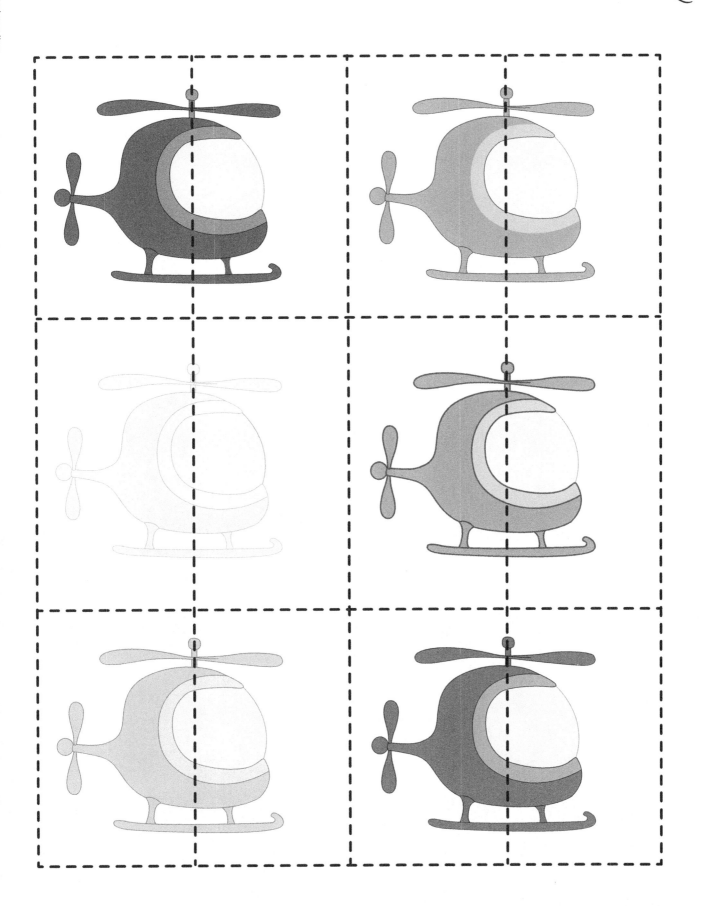

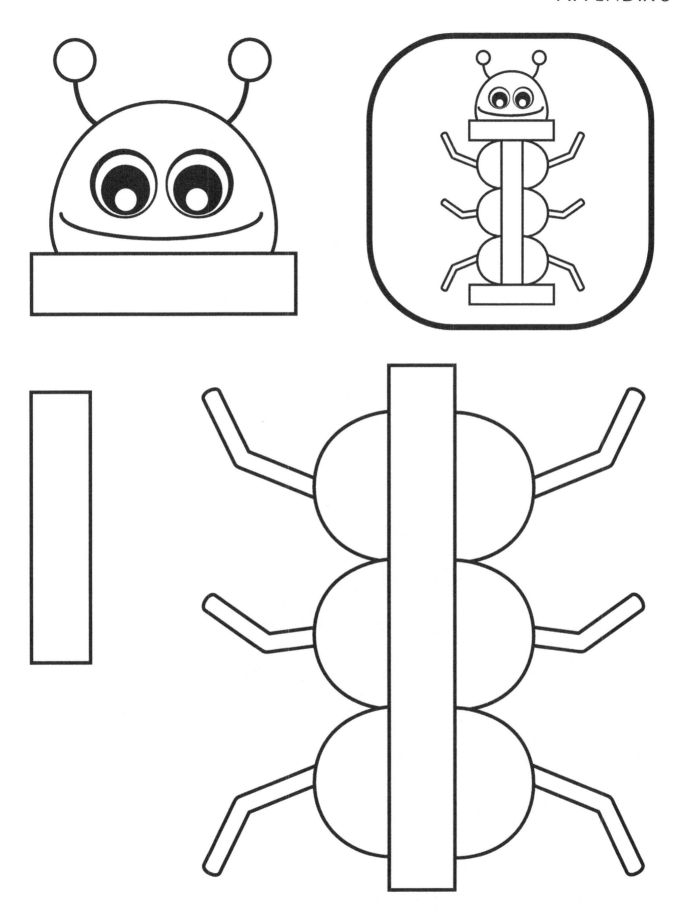

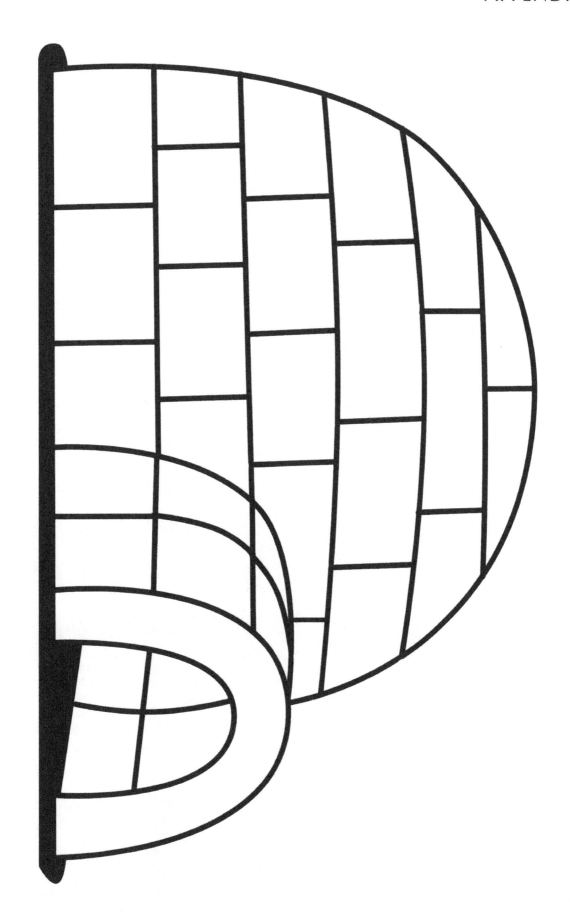

cut along line

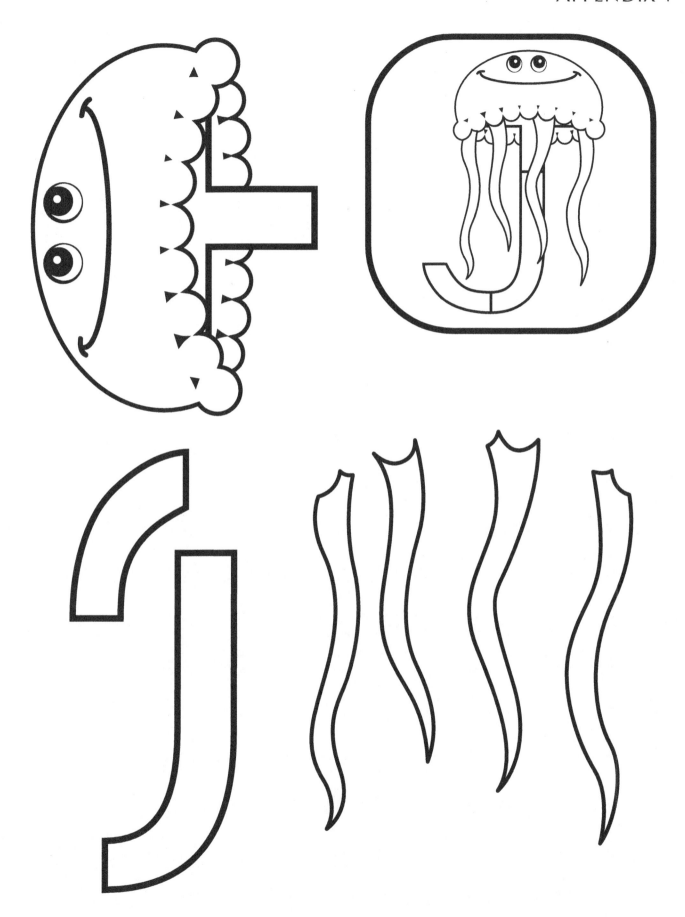

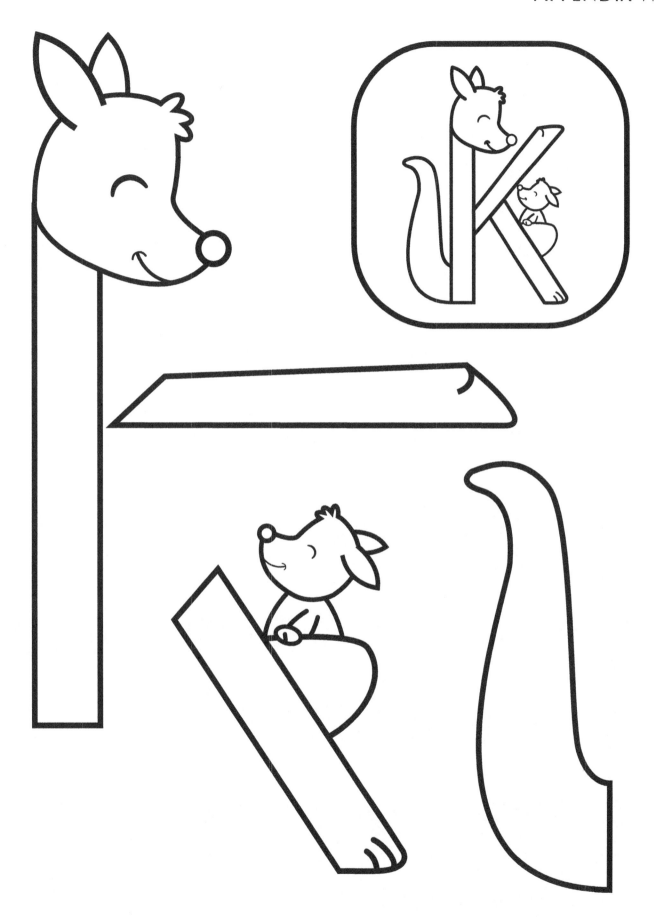

Toddler Lesson Plans: Learning ABC's | Autumn McKa

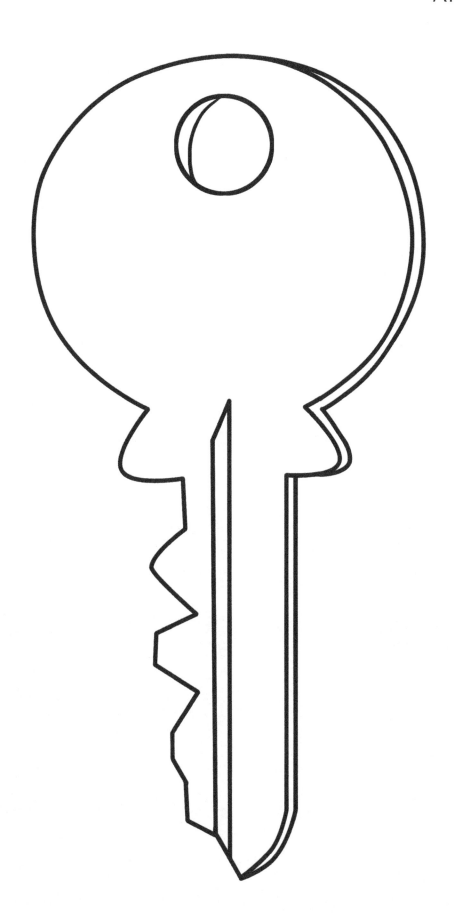

cut along line

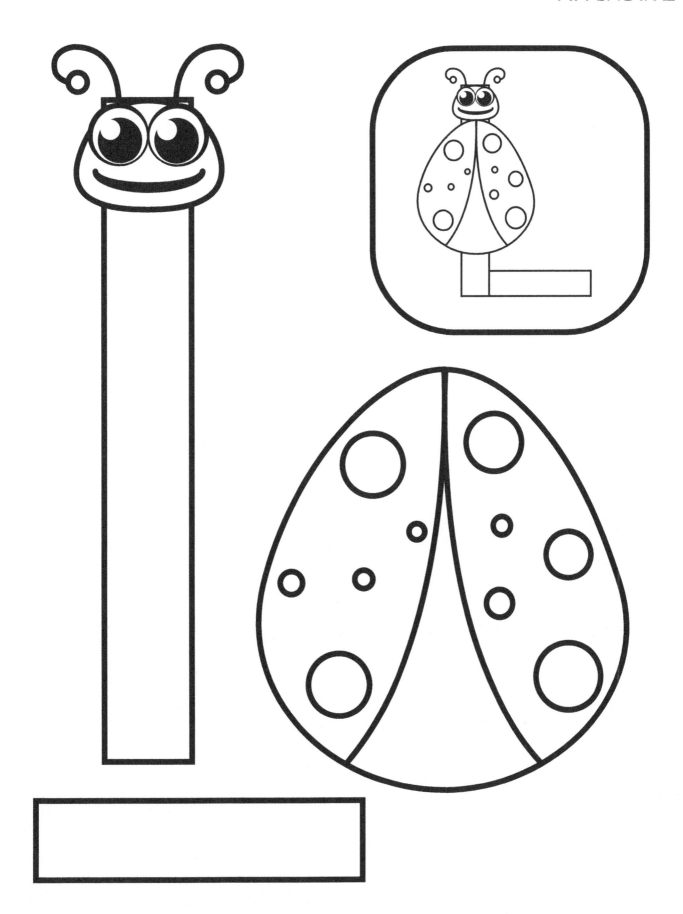

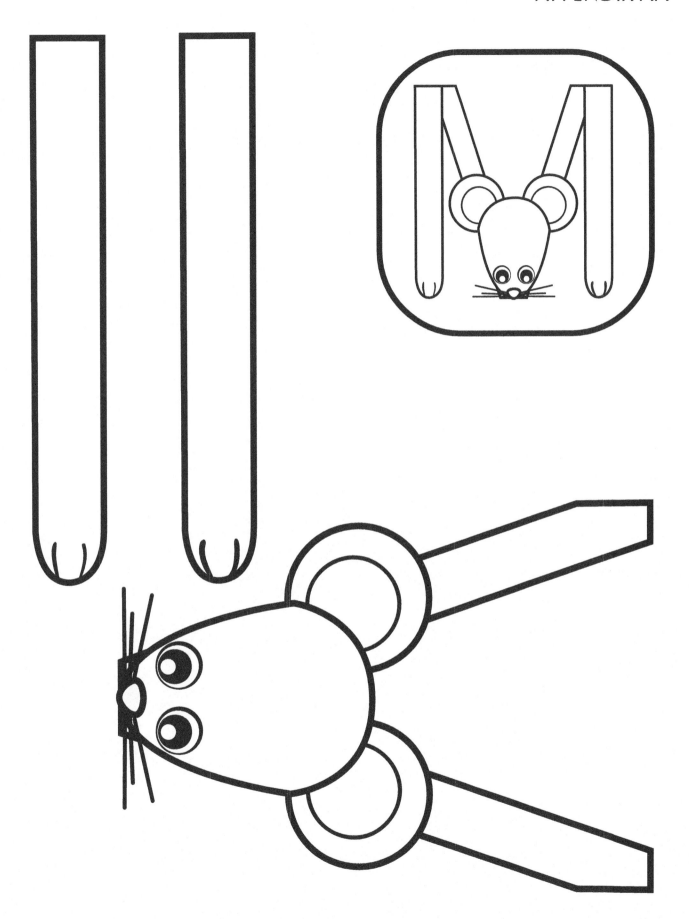

M & M Sorting

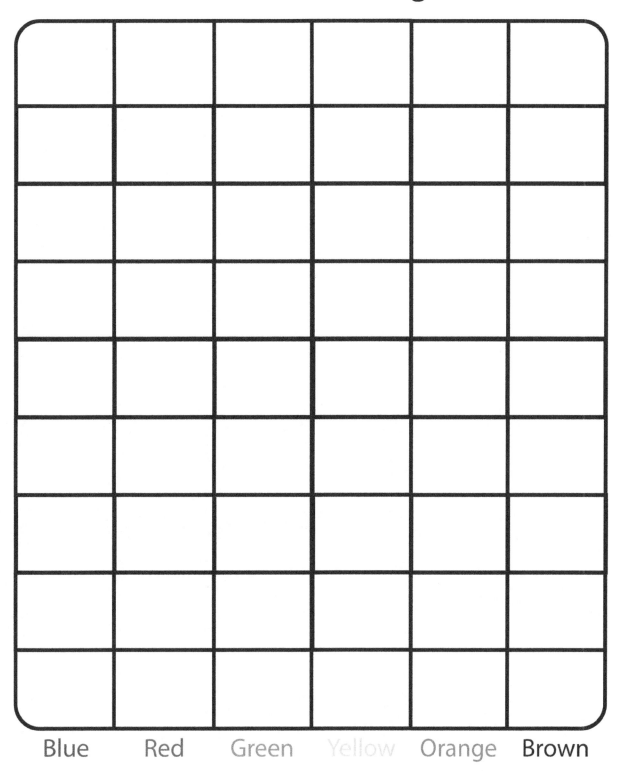

| Blue | Red | Green | Yellow | Orange | Brown |

cut along line

cut along line

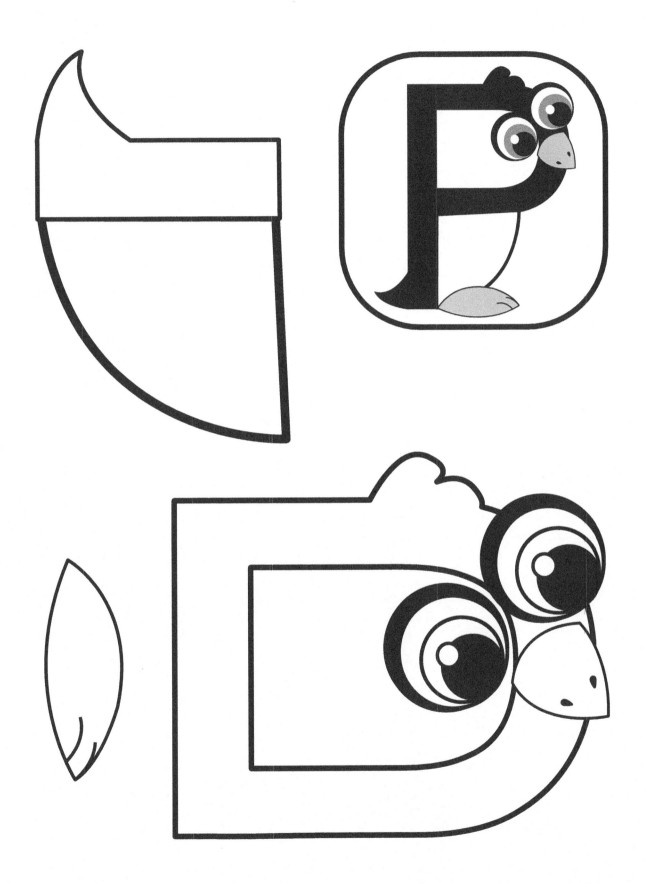

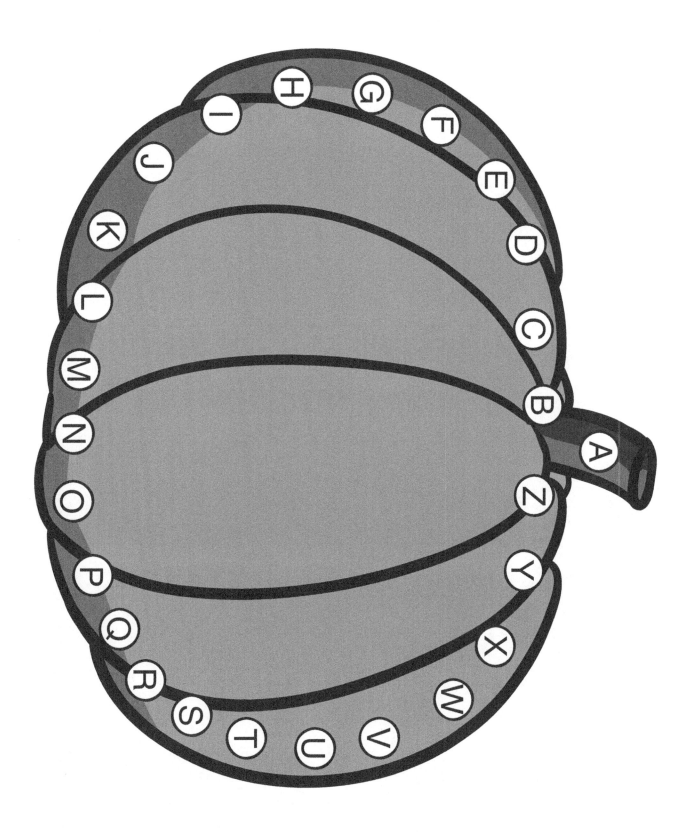

cut along line

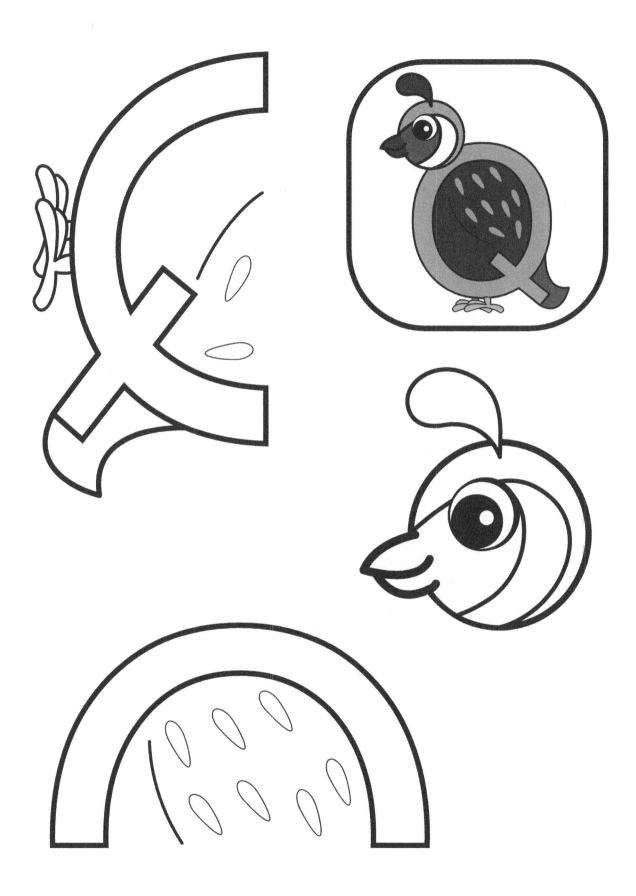

cut along line

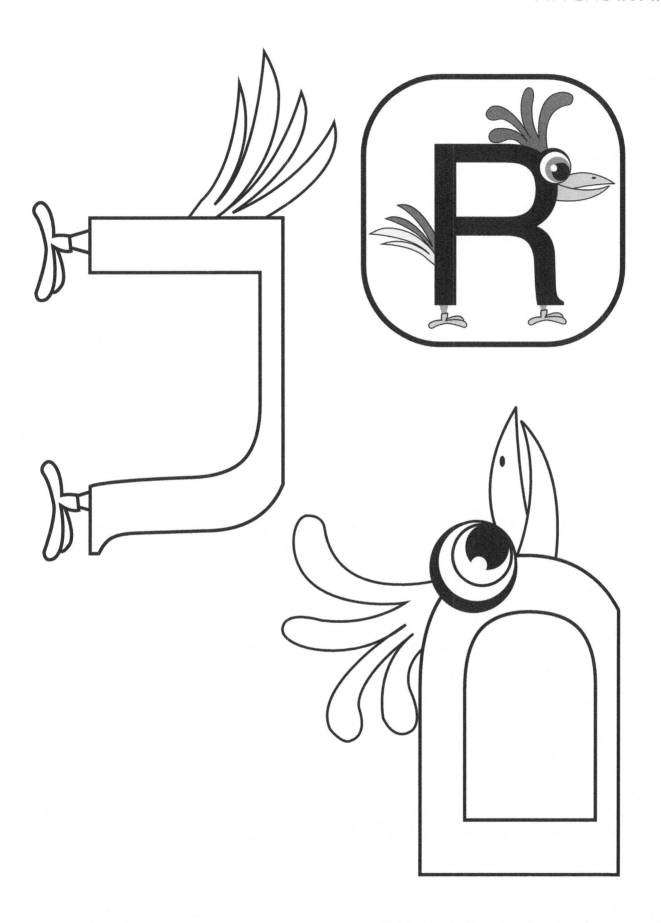

cut along line

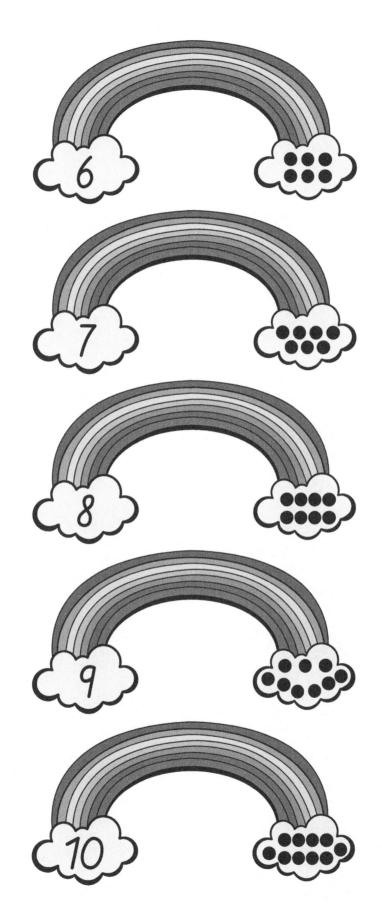

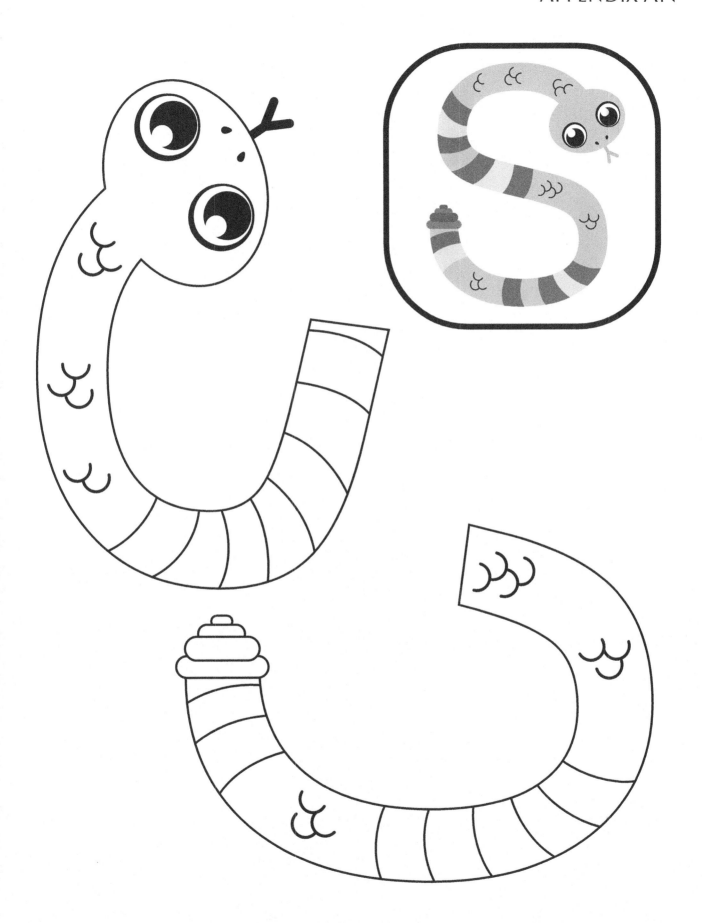

cut along line

cut along line

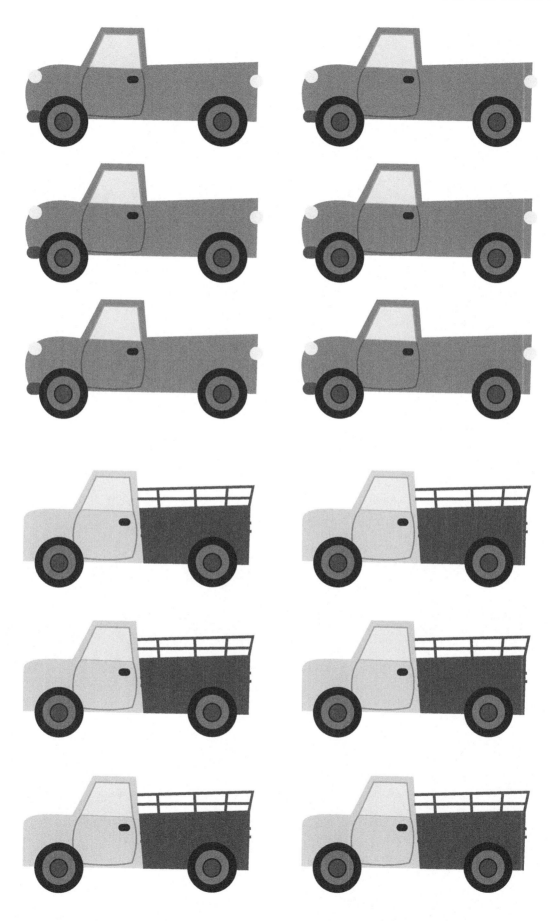

cut along line

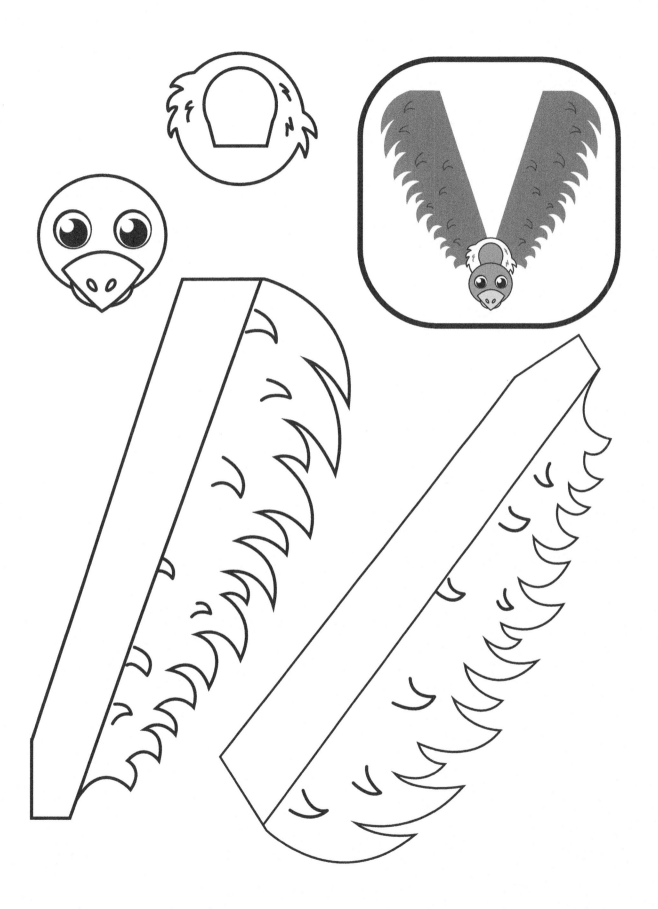

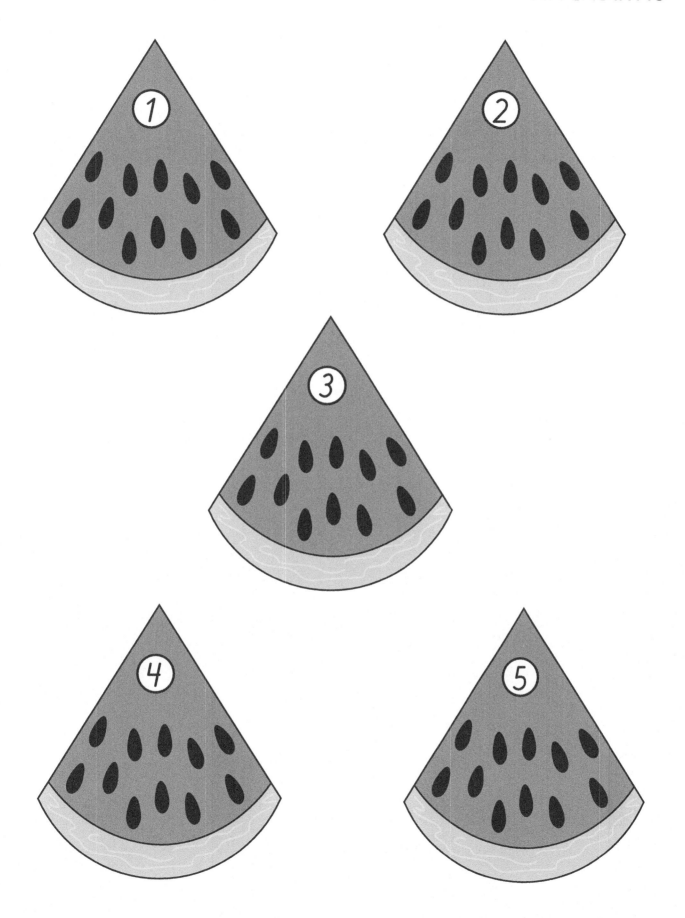

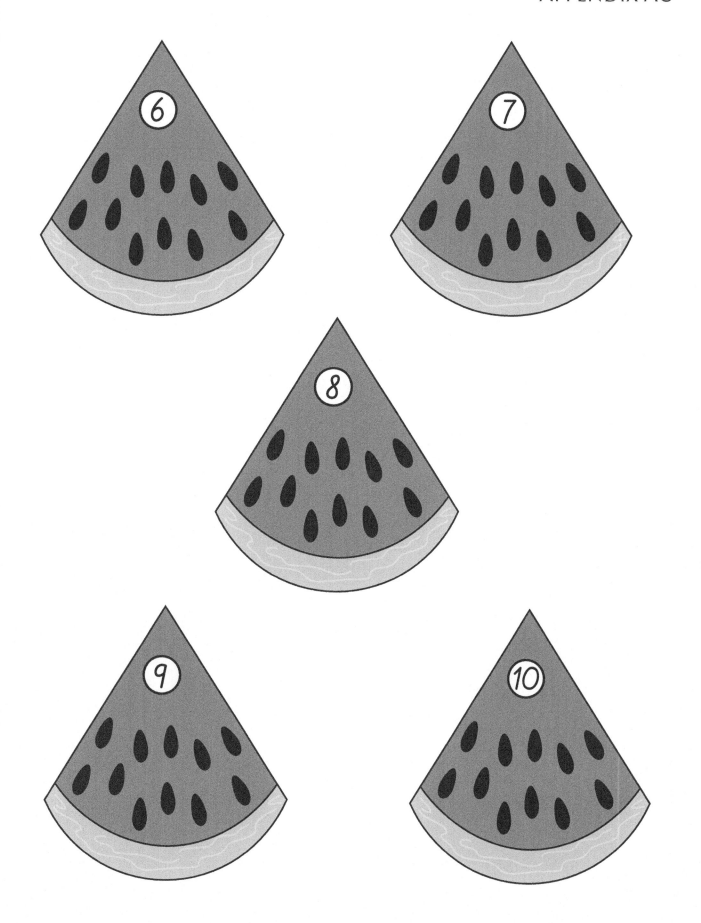

cut along line

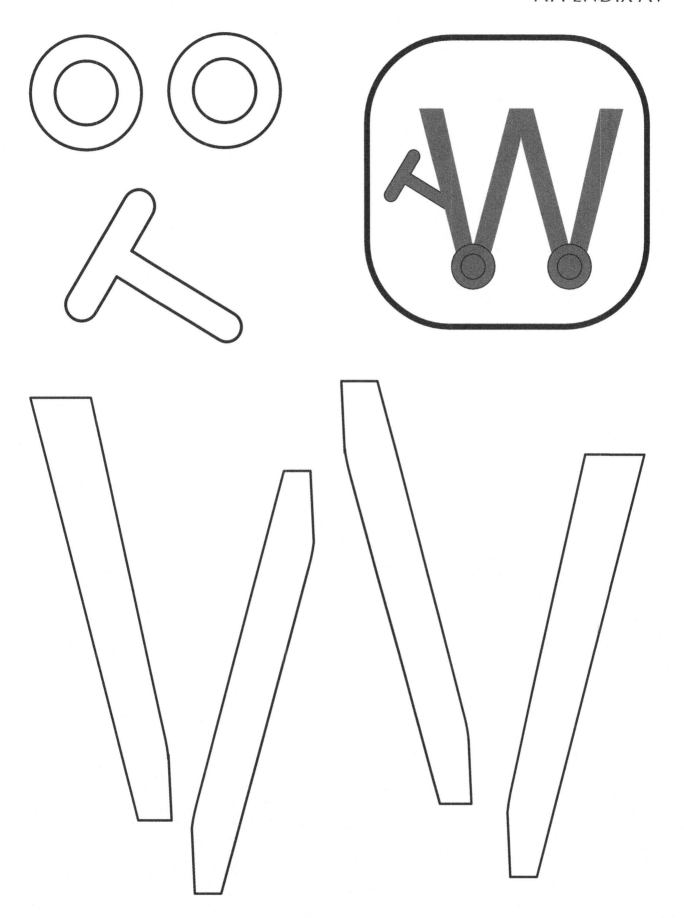

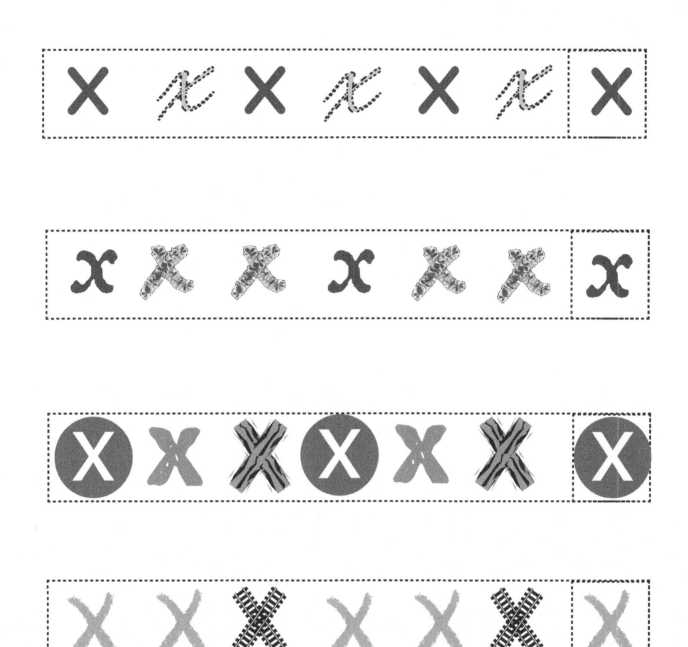

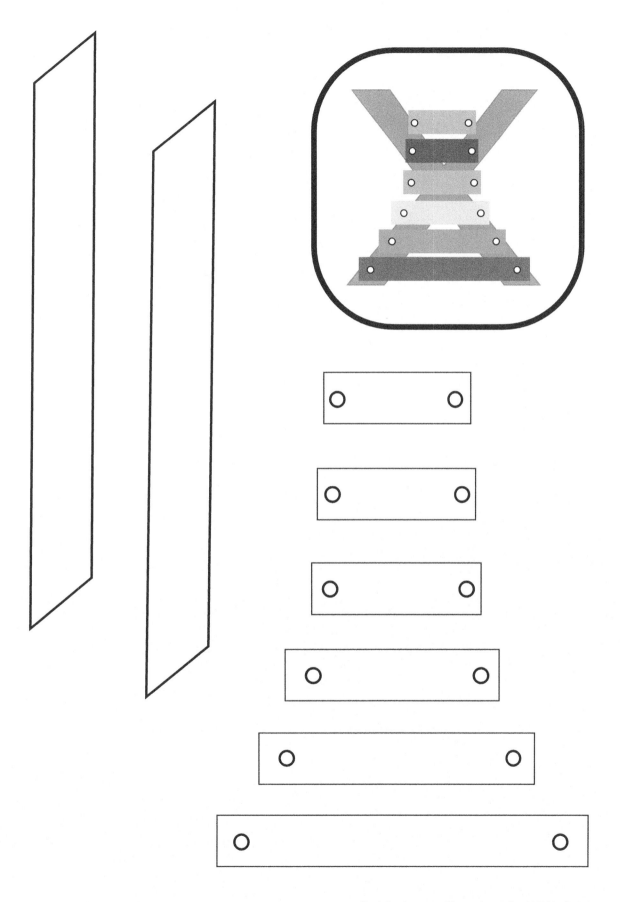

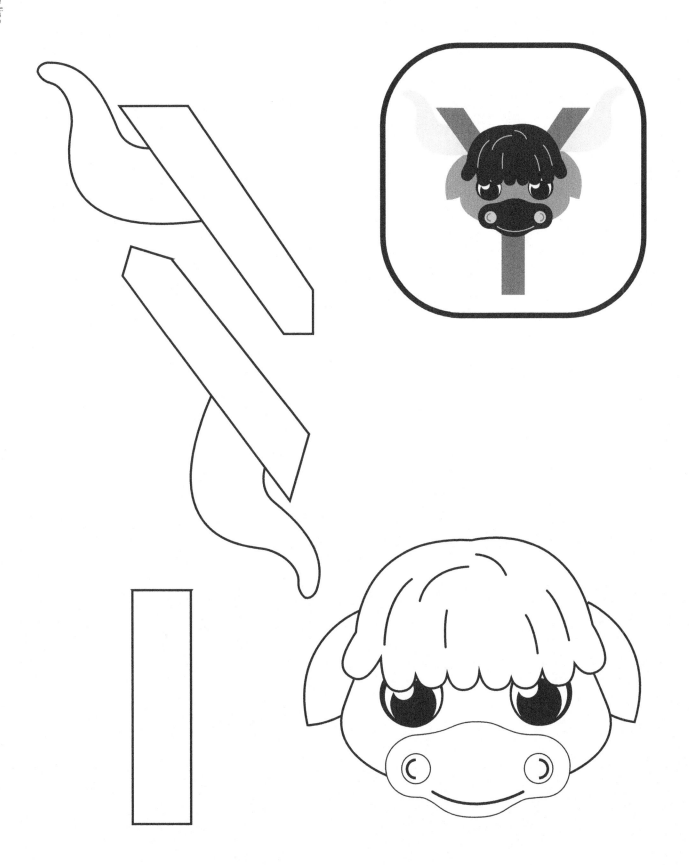

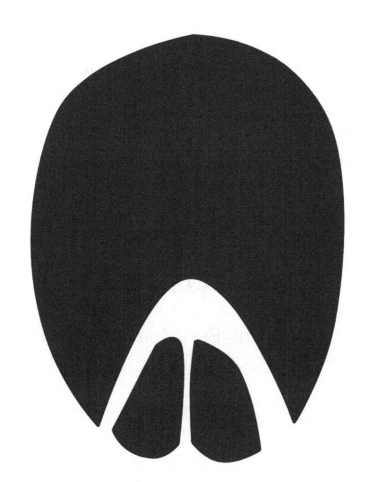

Thank you for welcoming me into your home!
I hope you and your child liked learning together with this book!

If you enjoyed this book, it would mean so much to me
if you wrote a review so other moms can learn from your
experience.

-♡-
Autumn

Autumn@BestMomIdeas.com

Discover Autumn's Other Books

Early Learning Series

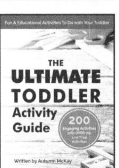
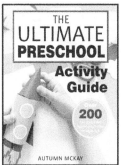

Early Learning Workbook Series

www.BestMomIdeas.com　　 @BestMomIdeas　　Best Mom Ideas